OFFICE FOR STANDARDS
IN EDUCATION

HOMEWORK
Learning from practice

Penelope Weston

LONDON: THE STATIONERY OFFICE

Office for Standards in Education
Alexandra House
33 Kingsway
London WC2B 6SE

Telephone 0171-421 6800

ISBN 0 11 350104 8

Contents

INTRODUCTION   **7**

1 THE SCOPE AND PURPOSE OF HOMEWORK   **11**

1.1   What Counts as Homework?   11

     Secondary schools   11
     Primary schools   12

1.2   The Purpose of Homework   14

1.3   The Status of Homework   17

     Setting expectations   17
     Integrating homework into the learning programme   18

1.4   Overview: Scope, Purpose and Status of Homework   19

2 HOMEWORK AND EFFECTIVE LEARNING: FORGING THE LINK   **21**

2.1   The Range of Tasks and Approaches   21

     Homework tasks   21
     Dimensions of homework   23

2.2   Planning   26

     Creating general frameworks   26
     Planning for content-linked topics, themes or units   27
     Planning with parents and pupils   28
     The benefits and costs of planning   29

2.3   Matching Homework to Pupils' Capabilities   30

     Differentiating homework   31
     Meeting special needs   32

2.4   Assessment and feedback   34

     The assessment framework   34
     Giving feedback: meaning and manageability   36

2.5   Purposeful Learning in English and Mathematics: Primary Experience   38

     Reading, writing, listening and speaking   38
     Numeracy and mathematical understanding   41

2.6   Overview: Towards High Quality Homework   42

3	**MANAGING THE HOMEWORK PROGRAMME**	**47**
3.1	How Much Homework?	47
	Time allocations	47
	Total time spent on homework: pupil reports	52
	Thinking about time	54
3.2	Managing the System	55
	Control and responsibilities	56
	Procedures and protocols	59
3.3	Steering the Strategy	67
	The policy and its purpose	67
	From policy to whole-school strategy: strategic planning, review and co-ordination	71
3.4	Investing in Homework	74
	Resourcing the regular programme	74
	Developing additional homework-related initiatives	77
3.5	Overview: The Well-Managed Homework Programme	81
4	**HOMEWORK MATTERS: IMPACT ON PUPILS, PARENTS AND SCHOOLS**	**85**
4.1	Perspectives on Practice: Pupils and Parents	85
	Pupils: approach, challenges, evaluation	85
	Parents' perceptions and involvement: primary schools	91
4.2	The Impact of Homework: Teachers' Judgements	93
4.3	Overview: The Impact of Homework	96
5	**LEARNING THROUGH PRACTICE: IMPLICATIONS OF THE STUDY**	**99**
5.1	Developing Good Homework Practice: Implications for Schools	99
	Foundations	99
	Integration with learning	101
	System management	103
	Strategic development	103
5.2	The Future of Homework	105
APPENDIX A	**METHODOLOGY**	**109**
A.1	Research review	109
A.2	Survey of schools	109
A.3	Case study visits	109
A.4	Pupil Questionnaire	110

APPENDIX B   THE RESEARCH AND POLICY CONTEXT   111

B.1   Research on Homework   111

     The purpose of homework and its relevance   111
       for learning

     The amount and type of homework allocated   112
       and reported

     Managing the process of homework   115

     Resources and conditions for homework,   115
       including parental support

     The impact of homework on learning and   117
       achievement

B.2   The Policy Context   119

B.3   Overview: Current thinking on Homework   121

REFERENCES   **122**

ACKNOWLEDGEMENTS

This report has been made possible by the support and co-operation of many groups and individuals. First and foremost come the staff and pupils of all the schools who took the trouble to provide the evidence on which the report is based, particularly the case study schools where teachers, pupils and some parents spent time talking about homework and supplying examples of what they had achieved. The visits were undertaken by a hardworking and highly experienced team whose expertise and insights were evident from the quality of their reports and the wealth of material they collected. The report also relied on the work of the team at Diagnostics Social and Market Research, led by Chrissie Wells, who carried out the telephone survey and analysed the findings. Further analyses were carried out by Ian Schagen, chief statistician of the National Foundation for Educational Research, who, with his colleagues, undertook the processing and analysis of the pupil survey; we are very grateful for this contribution. The review of research literature on homework was also carried out at NFER, by Caroline Sharp, and her work was extremely valuable in providing a foundation for his inquiry. The third NFER contribution came from Dr Wendy Keys whose comments on the draft were most helpful and to the point. Further recent research evidence was kindly provided by David Lambert of London University and Mike Johnson of Keele University.

Throughout the study, I have received the continuing support of the OFSTED research team, led by Christine Agambar; I should like to thank them for their help, with a particular tribute to David Read who has responded to all queries and challenges with imperturbable good humour and efficiency.

INTRODUCTION

In recent years homework has come to the fore, as a topic with new interest for schools, parents and politicians. Who should do homework? How much should they do? What kind of tasks should be included? And above all, how can it help children to make progress?

The study reported here has been carried out by, and on behalf of, OFSTED, for the Department for Education and Employment (DfEE). The findings are intended to '*reflect and take account of best current practice*' and to be of direct use to schools as a resource in interpreting the Government's national guidelines. It has arisen out of the Government's interest in homework as an integral element of learning, as set out in the 1997 White Paper, *Excellence in Schools*:

> *Homework is not an optional extra, but an essential part of a good education. There is clear evidence that it helps pupils - in particular those from disadvantaged backgrounds - reach higher standards. It also allows more effective use to be made of lesson times and improves pupils' study skills and attitudes to learning. Parents should know what homework their children are expected to do and the support they themselves should give. The school's approach to homework is expected to be one of the key elements of its home-school contract....*
>
> *The amount and type of homework pupils do cannot continue to be left to chance. The enormous inconsistencies between schools mean that hundreds of thousands of primary children are missing out on opportunities to build on what they learn in the classroom. We intend to ensure that all schools - and all pupils - are helped and challenged to live up to the high standards set by the best.*

The White Paper went on to explain that the Government planned to issue national guidelines on homework, covering:

- *how much homework pupils of different ages should do;*

- *how much time pupils of different ages should spend on homework;*

- *what sort of tasks and activities make good homework;*

- *how schools can develop and implement successful homework policies; and*

- *what is expected of both schools and parents.*

This study was commissioned at a stage when thinking about the guidelines had only just begun. In practice, evidence from the study contributed to the development of the national guidelines, first issued for consultation in April 1998.

This report brings together evidence on homework practice from a number of strands of which the study was composed:

1 **Telephone surveys** of homework practice in 368 schools (primary and secondary);

2 **Case study visits** to 29 selected primary and secondary schools, to interview teachers, parents and pupils;

3 **Questionnaire survey of pupils** from schools visited in (2);

4 **Review of recent research on homework**, carried out by the National Foundation for Educational Research (Sharp, 1997);

5 **Analysis of the replies** to the homework questions in the consultation on the 1997 White Paper *Excellence in Schools*.

Strands 1 to 3 constitute the main investigation, based on data collected specifically for this study, and provide the evidence for the remaining chapters. A summary of the research methods used for the investigation is given in Appendix A. Strands 4 and 5 complement the research evidence, showing what is known about homework through systematic inquiry (Strand 4) and professional judgement (Strand 5). Findings from these two strands can be found in Appendix B.

The new investigations commissioned for this study were based on current practice in a range of primary and secondary schools which had already been judged by OFSTED to offer effective homework policies and provision. Samples for the telephone survey (Strand 1) and case studies (Strand 2) were drawn from lists of schools inspected under the new inspection framework, since June 1996, and the selection was based on high ratings for quality of homework practice (where available) or on overall ratings for teaching and learning. By definition, therefore, these schools had been judged to have good practice. The investigations carried out for this study made it possible to describe that practice in more detail, to explore the thinking behind it and to identify common features.

The agenda addressed by the study is wide ranging, covering the 5-16 age-range and a number of topics and areas:

- schools' homework **policies** and their implementation;

- the **amount** of homework set, and the **time spent** by pupils;

- the **type** of homework set (including issues relating to differentiation);

- homework **assessment and feedback**;

- **resource** implications of homework;

- **integration** of homework with classroom learning;

- use of **homework clubs** and **study support centres**;

- **pupil motivation** for homework.

The study was also expected to provide evidence on the contribution which an effective homework policy can make to:

- promoting **positive pupil attitudes to school**;

- enhancing **pupil achievement**;

- promoting **positive parental attitudes and involvement**.

The report is informed by certain criteria related to the aims of the study:

- **Current.** In keeping with the aims of the study, the focus is on current practice: principles, policies, programmes and procedures which are proving feasible in schools at this time. All the evidence was gathered during the 1997 autumn term and therefore reflects what schools are doing in the current policy context.

- **Appropriate.** The evidence covers both primary and secondary schools and includes schools in a wide range of settings, with differing characteristics. Clearly, solutions and requirements will vary according to the context.

- **Practicable.** By definition, all the strategies reviewed here, and any examples selected, are drawn from practice. As far as the evidence allows, every effort will be made to show the resources and planning involved in implementing these strategies.

- **Purposeful.** Homework is not an end in itself, or at least it is not intended to be, and it is important to evaluate the extent to which any strategy or programme contributes to the improvement of learning and achievement. Within the scope of a short-term study it was impossible to design research to test the impact of different homework programmes, but a number of checks can be made, not least the rigour with which the school evaluates the effectiveness of the programme.

- **Fair.** Does the homework programme meet the needs of all pupils: the most and least able, those with special needs, those with challenging or unconventional home circumstances? Does it take account of parents' need to be fully informed, of their capacity and willingness to be involved? Does it expect too much or too little of parents?

Each of the following chapters of the report will review one aspect of homework principles or practice. Chapter 1 asks about the purpose and scope of homework, as this is understood by teachers, pupils and parents. What counts as homework? What is it for? How important is it, and how does it fit into broader school policies, for example on home-school links, study skills and effective learning? In Chapter 2, the discussion moves from purpose to practice, to address the key issues of quality and effectiveness: what do teachers do to ensure that homework is making a real contribution to effective learning? The chapter looks at how teachers manage the planning, differentiation and assessment of homework, using evidence on homework practice in primary English and mathematics to illustrate these themes. Chapter 3 concentrates on schools' policies and procedures for managing their homework programme, including evidence on the quantity of homework expected and undertaken. Chapter 4 completes the discussion of evidence by reviewing the impact of homework on pupils, parents and schools. Finally, Chapter 5 considers the implications of the study, particularly for planners and managers.

Appendix A gives a summary of the research methods used to collect the evidence for this investigation. Appendix B uses the evidence from recent research and from the consultation responses to the White Paper to identify and discuss current issues and assumptions about homework. This sets the context for the report, which draws directly on the evidence collected for this study.

Each chapter takes account of practice in both primary and secondary schools. Indeed, it can be instructive to compare approaches in the two phases and to ask to what extent differences are necessary and appropriate. The central focus is on Key Stage 2 (KS2) and Key Stage 3 (KS3), the years when, for many pupils, homework practice becomes fully developed.

The study has shown that there are indeed a number of issues of principle and practice that will need to be clarified by each school community as it reviews its homework policy. Perhaps too much has been taken for granted - for example that all those involved share a common understanding about what homework is. However, it is also clear that there is good practice about; we found evidence of this in a number of schools which believed in the role which homework could play in pupils' success, evidence which will be presented in later chapters of this report. Moreover, thinking about homework, and about the role it can play in pupils' learning, is developing fast. We hope this report will contribute to that process.

1 The Scope and Purpose of Homework

This is the first of four chapters which draw on the evidence collected directly for this study, from teachers (through the telephone survey and the case studies), from pupils (though a questionnaire and discussions in the case study schools) and from parents (through discussions in the case study primary schools). Details of all these data sources are given in Appendix A. **It should be remembered in this and following chapters that, as explained in the introduction, the survey and case study schools were all selected because they had received a good rating from OFSTED, either specifically for homework or for teaching and learning generally.** The findings therefore reflect 'good practice' and do not necessarily represent what happens in all schools.

This chapter explores the scope and purpose of homework, as seen by the schools in the study. It is apparently fairly easy to get agreement at a general level from parents and teachers on the 'value' of homework and this has perhaps encouraged the view that its nature and purpose are understood, shared and non-problematic. In fact, the assumptions, and the lists of purposes for homework to be found in policy documents, have developed mainly from secondary school practice and priorities. The recent growth of homework in primary schools in this country has highlighted less familiar aspects of the agenda: for example the part which homework can play in developing home-school relations, informing parents about the curriculum and teaching methods and thus encouraging their more active involvement and collaboration. The chapter begins (1.1) with a discussion of how homework is defined in each school phase and goes on to look at the purposes which schools define for it (1.2). The review then considers the status of homework (in relation to class work) and its place within the overall school strategy (1.3).

1.1 What Counts as Homework?

Nearly all the 141 secondary schools (96%) and over three-quarters of the 227 primary schools (78%) which took part in the telephone survey on homework had a written homework policy and over 200 sent these in as part of the study. In the case study schools[1] we were able to inspect policy documents in many cases and discuss them with staff. These documents were one place to look for the school's own official definition of homework. In the case study schools we could also ask teachers themselves for their interpretation.

Secondary schools

Most secondary schools, where homework is a long-established tradition, tend to assume, understandably, that no definition of homework is needed. Only one of the ten secondary schools visited for this study provided a definition of homework (for parents of KS4 pupils): '*work set to be done outside the classroom and not under staff supervision*'. It was more common, in homework policies and guidelines for parents, to launch straight into the reasons for setting homework and the procedures for managing it. There might be a discussion of the range of work involved. Some school guidelines made it clear to parents that, since they were at school, there had been major changes in the kind of tasks which might be set for homework; in this way they provided a working definition (see Box 1.1) of the range of tasks currently involved. But this does not resolve other questions about the boundaries between 'homework' and school work.

In the secondary context, one challenge for those providing guidance is that not all homework is done at home; in fact, for some pupils who find it hard to work at home, or for some tasks which may require resources (books, software, equipment) more readily available at school, it is necessary or desirable to carry out the task at school. One school solved the problem by replacing the term 'homework' with 'personal study'. One advantage of doing so was that the term could apply equally to a Year 7 book review or the

---

1   Ten secondary schools and 19 primary schools agreed to act as case studies. In keeping with normal research conventions, they will not be named in the report.

**BOX 1.1
HOMEWORK MEANINGS AND PURPOSES**

This technology college was inspected in May 1996 and received a very positive report. However, inconsistent practice in setting homework in KS3 was highlighted as a key issue for action. Since then the school has tackled this issue with vigour. A sub-group of the Curriculum Committee was given the task, and first clarified what homework was (by listing the forms it can take) and the purposes it should serve. Their conclusions were presented in the form of clear and simple checklists (see below), designed to be useful for pupils, parents and teachers. Each department is required to produce its own more detailed policy to comply with these criteria

HOMEWORK	**HOMEWORK**
What form can it take?	**What is it for?**
• learning	• independent learning
• reading	• consolidation
• writing	• practice - learning by doing
• research	• completion of course work assignments
• interviews	
• watching/observing	• self-discipline
• drawing	• research
• tape-recording	• pupil/parent/teacher partnership
• word-processing	• work not suited to classroom situation

preparation of GCSE course work or an A level essay. Others explained to parents that their child might genuinely have done the work during the school day. The assumption here, and in most other guidelines written by secondary schools, is that 'homework' is essentially independent study, carried out by the pupil outside the timetabled lesson, without the direct support of the teacher; and that in most cases it will be done at home, with parental backing (but probably not direct involvement). However, no such definition is watertight. For example, departments in some schools provided regular sessions when subject teachers voluntarily provided support at lunch time or after schools to pupils who asked for it and, as we shall see later, there were differing views about how parents should help with homework at the secondary stage.

Primary schools

From the primary school perspective, homework can look rather different. Most schools taking part in this study were clear that sustained written tasks undertaken by Year 6 pupils, often in the core subjects, were undoubtedly 'homework' and these were often consciously designed to prepare pupils for the perceived demands of the secondary school homework programme. But some schools distinguished explicitly between what they called 'formal homework' of this kind and the ongoing regular learning and practice tasks expected of primary pupils of all ages: reading, spelling, number bonds and multiplication tables. Others started from a very different viewpoint, focusing on all the learning children do out of school, often with their parents, and seeking to strengthen and reinforce this. Such a broad approach was seen as particularly appropriate for KS1. As one primary school put it, for this age group '*homework could be any activity which will encourage the social skills of sharing and co-operation*'. In response to the telephone survey, many schools sent copies of their homework policies, showing how they addressed this issue of what counts as homework. One of these made an explicit distinction between all the general and specific activities to support learning which were termed 'work at home' and, within this, 'homework' tasks which seemed to consist mainly of written language assignments for Years 5 and 6. Another, which had a very detailed reading policy specifying how parents could help and also expected pupils to learn spellings and tables, nevertheless said they had no 'formal homework'. One school offered a clear definition in their policy, again coming up with a new label as well:

Homework is work which is set to be done outside the timetabled curriculum but not necessarily at home. It does contain an element of independent study in that it is not usually directly supervised or controlled by a teacher and it represents an extension of the learning activities provided and organised in accordance with the objectives of the School curriculum. Since one of the purposes of schooling is to enable pupils to learn independently of the School, the term 'home learning' is more appropriate than homework.

This definition raises questions about how 'independent' the pupil's work at home should be. For almost all primary schools with a homework programme, the contribution which parents can make, especially in the early years, was recognised as enormous and essential. Over and over again, staff spoke of homework as a partnership between teacher, parent and child, so that it was essentially a co-operative venture. Some schools provided simple games which parents (or indeed older siblings) could play with the child to encourage counting and classifying skills. For some, this kind of activity was certainly 'homework'; others would have seen it as 'normal' parental activity. While it was widely agreed that the parental role changed as the child got older, with more encouragement and less direct involvement, the difference in outlook between primary and secondary schools on this point was exemplified in one urban primary school by a request from the local secondary school that Year 6 pupils should receive 'no parental help' with homework. Other schools stressed the importance of maintaining parental involvement in some activities, for example reading to and with Year 5 and 6 children.

There was also the issue of whether homework was an essential part of the learning programme. The great majority of primary schools in our sample expected it to apply to all pupils on the grounds that if it was valuable for some then it was valuable for all. But in some schools there was a less inclusive approach, with homework apparently given to supplement learning for those seen to need this extra input (for example, when a child would benefit from extra practice, had been absent, or needed resources not found in school). One urban multi-ethnic primary school in an area of poor housing recognised the difficulties which some children faced at home but nevertheless considered that homework was actually a way of compensating for poor home background. Even when the opportunity to enhance learning through homework was offered to all, some primary school homework policies made clear that doing it was voluntary. A rural first school saw homework as a matter of encouragement and using opportunities.

Those primary schools with homework policies did not generally provide a definition, perhaps because this might vary according to age, but one junior school policy document spelled it out in a checklist:

Within the Primary School years we see homework embracing a wide range of activities, occasions and events which include many of the following at various times:

- *weekly learning of tables (at ability level)*

- *weekly learning of spellings (at ability level and the context of current work)*

- *reading to a family member or listening to a family member reading*

- *family visits to local museums, farms etc., reinforcing aspects of current classroom studies*

- *completion of assignments during weekend or holiday periods in relation to Topic Studies*

- *involvement in activities such as: sports clubs, cubs, brownies, dancing, choir*

- *music instrument practice*

- *the school's programme of wide-ranging extra-curricular activities*

While all these were mentioned somewhere in our study in connection with homework, not all schools would be happy with such an all-inclusive list which blurs the boundaries between school-initiated and home-initiated activities.

Since it was anticipated that primary schools might differ in their definitions of homework, the telephone survey started with its own:

In this interview, you should take homework to mean all tasks that pupils are asked to carry out at home, including, for instance, reading to parents.

On this basis, it was clear that all schools selected for the survey, primary as well as secondary, organised homework for all the age groups (if not necessarily all pupils) in their school.

Definitions -explicit or implicit - are likely to relate to what the school sees as the purpose of homework, an area on which there was much more evidence.

1.2 The Purpose of Homework

Most homework policies submitted in this study started with a rationale, setting out the aims and objectives for homework, the reasons for doing it or its place in the broader teaching and learning policy. The underlying argument was that effective homework would help to raise attainment. The purposes listed tended to focus on several main aspects, e.g. :

- consolidation/reinforcement: learning facts/concepts, practising skills;

- creating more time: to finish off work, read around, draft;

- homework as discipline: time/self management, independent work;

- home/school links: to involve/'educate' parents, two-way channel;

- enrichment: learning is fun, worthwhile, part of real life, chance to develop new skills.

During the telephone interview, the senior teachers involved in the survey were asked to put forward the main purposes for homework in their school, as they saw them. These were then categorised, and Figure 1.1 shows the purposes suggested by at least 10% of one of the two groups (primary and secondary schools). Interestingly, 'raising attainment' was not explicitly mentioned, though some spoke of helping the children to reach their potential. What seemed to be important were the more specific objectives which might contribute to better performance.

The figure shows that both groups saw the consolidation of skills taught in class as one of the main purposes of homework, but there were clear differences between primary and secondary schools in the other purposes most often mentioned. The second priority for primary head teachers was that homework should promote home-school partnership, and indeed help parents to become more closely involved in their child's education.

This idea was spelled out in their documents:

Teachers recognise that homework has greater success when it is valued by pupils and parents. We believe that it is important that

Figure 1.1
Primary and Secondary Managers' Definitions of the Purpose of Homework

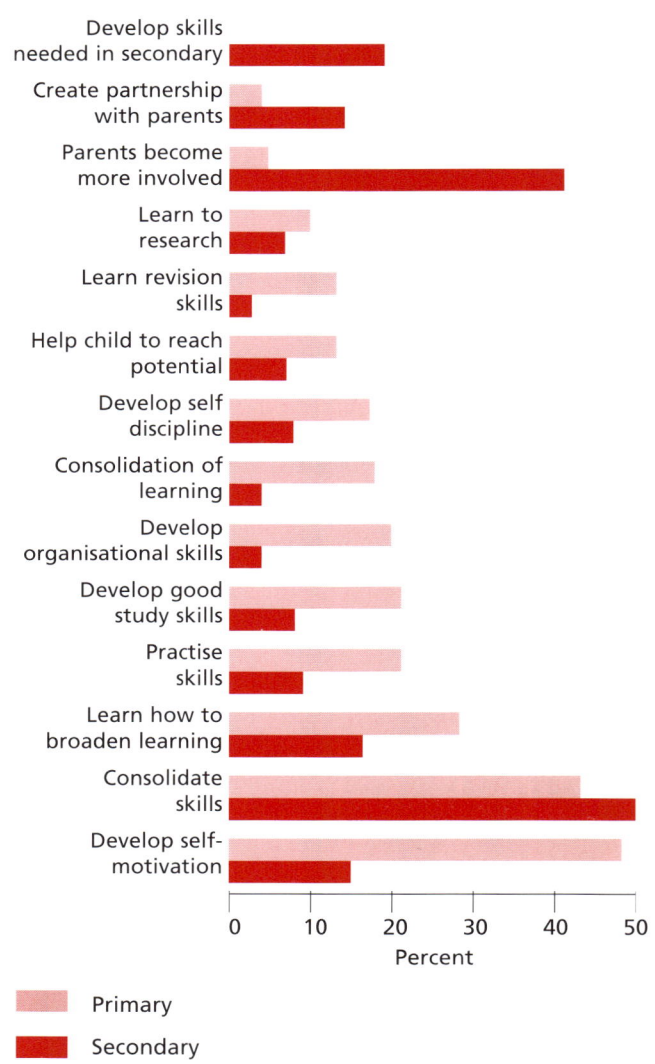

Source: Diagnostics Telephone Survey of 227 Primary and 141 Secondary Schools, October 1997.

children bring 'work' home from a fairly young age so that links between home and school can be developed and enhanced.

3-11 school

One of the school's aims is 'to promote a close liaison between home and school..' By setting homework for our pupils we hope to involve parents more in their children's education, to increase parents' understanding of the work being done in school, to improve the feedback for parents about their children's progress and to extend and reinforce work covered in school.

First school

At ...... School we believe regular homework enables parents and other interested parties to become closely involved with children's learning and school work.

5-11 Primary

However, for one junior school parental involvement had moved to the end of the list:

Why we feel homework is important:

- *to develop further good work habits and independent study skills*

- *to develop further a self-disciplining and self-motivating attitude to study*

- *to practise and reinforce skills learned in the classroom*

- *to consolidate and extend work begun in the classroom*

- *to enhance study by making greater use of materials and sources of information which may not be available in the classroom e.g. visit the local library*

- *to involve parents (and other adults) in children's work*

As we shall see in later chapters, many primary schools backed up these principles with initiatives to involve parents actively with homework.

For secondary schools, a wider range of purposes was put forward overall in the telephone survey, with each respondent suggesting an average of three or four purposes (compared with the primary school group who mostly suggested one or two). There was a strong emphasis on the role of homework in developing the motivation and skills needed for independent learning. As some staff and policies explained, the demands of GCSE course work meant that it was essential for pupils to develop the self-discipline and study skills for sustained work from Year 7 onwards. In other words, homework was not just for practising and reinforcing what had been taught, but actually for developing and using additional skills which would become increasingly important as pupils grew older. If this was really the case, it had implications for the kind of tasks to be set for homework and for the way in which the purposes were put over to pupils.

Visits to schools as part of the study confirmed these priorities but also raised new issues. There appeared to be differences in many schools between the 'official' or head's version and the priorities of class teachers, pupils, parents. This might be a difference of emphasis, linked to the speaker's perspective. For example, at one primary school with a very clear policy document, the head-teacher stressed that the main purpose of homework was to get the parents involved so that they knew what work their child was covering, while class teachers saw homework as mainly supporting work in class and reinforcement. At another primary, the teachers were more also more pragmatic than the head, stressing the need to prepare children for secondary school and using homework as an opportunity for some pupils to finish off work they had not completed in class. As the researcher commented, the headteacher's aims were more strategic and concerned with the school's ethos, while the teachers' aims were more practical, looking at the direct influence on learning and progress. In general, however, primary staff were agreed about the purpose of homework, perhaps because the policy had often been developed by the whole staff team. In secondary schools it was more challenging to achieve this kind of unity of purpose. In one grammar school seven reasons for homework were listed in the guidelines for parents, but for the staff there were really three: to extend the learning week, to assess pupils' knowledge and to complete class work.

The issue of 'finishing off' shows up most clearly the tension which can arise between the official goals and classroom practice. Was it one of the approved purposes of homework to allow slower pupils to complete class work? In some schools this was seen as legitimate (Reason 6 out of 7: *It gives them time to complete work not finished in class*. Grammar school, Guidelines for Parents), although often 'finishing off' was restricted to 'occasional' use. In its homework policy, a suburban primary school with an extensive homework programme presented 'finishing off' as an additional task:

Please note that class work not completed during school time will be sent home for completion to be handed in the following day.

One secondary school in the survey clearly explained the problem in its policy statement:

Staff are asked where appropriate to tailor homework to the needs of the individual pupil so as to stretch the brightest and support the weakest. This means, for example, not regularly setting work which just asks pupils to 'finish off what we started in class...' as this results in the most able pupils getting a very easy ride, and the slowest being well and truly lumbered!

For many teachers, however, using homework to complete class work was both acceptable and indeed necessary, whatever the policy said. For example, in one 11 to 16 school staff said this was the only way they could keep the whole class together. In other cases, it was common (if unauthorised) practice. Thus in a comprehensive school with a clear written homework policy and rigorous procedures for seeing it was set, completed and marked, the apparent lack of a clear and shared understanding amongst staff of the purposes of homework helped to explain the gap between policy and practice. The researcher noted a very routine 'finish off your class work' approach which seemed to be the staple diet in most subjects, and which pupils found unmotivating.

What emerged from all the evidence on the purposes of homework, gathered from senior managers and other teachers, was that senior managers, especially those who had invested time and energy in developing a homework strategy, often had a broad and strategic view of the purpose of homework, seeing it as an opportunity to develop and broaden learning skills and even to lay the foundations of lifelong learning. This involved, especially in the early years, the closest partnership with parents; indeed, a number of schools defined them formally as 'co-educators'. For senior managers this meant that homework could serve a valuable secondary purpose of 'educating' parents about the curriculum and teaching methods. For many class and subject teachers, the purposes of homework were likely to be seen in more practical terms. Some schools had clearly closed this gap between a strategic and a more pragmatic view of homework.

What were the indicators that a school had achieved a consensus on the scope and purpose of homework? One clear measure was a fit between policy and practice. A new primary head was pleased to find, in the first few weeks, that the staff, parents and pupils were saying and doing just what the documents on homework had led her to expect. From the schools in this study certain principles emerged about the factors which show this is happening:

- **Clear leadership and consultation by the senior managers**. The homework policy has been actively developed in full consultation with the rest of the staff and indeed with parents, often over a sustained period.

- **Homework as part of the overall mission**. Homework is presented as part of the overall learning strategy, 'embedded' in classroom practice, and in line with the school ethos.

- **Consistency.** The purposes are known and understood by all teachers and pupils and also by parents; and observed in practice.

- **Reinforcement.** Many methods are used for getting the message home, especially to parents and pupils, e.g. simple guidelines appropriate to their audience, workshops, termly letters, in-service training, monitoring of practice.

One challenge in developing such agreement was the feeling that pupils' circumstances had to be taken into account in the rationale for homework, including their age, ability and home context. The telephone survey and indeed the school visits showed how priorities, if not purposes, changed according to the age of the pupils. About 60% of the telephone survey schools, in each phase, said homework purposes were the same for all year groups. The remaining primary heads stressed the need to strengthen reading skills and build greater parental involvement in the early years, with more independent, 'research'-oriented work in later years. Some also felt that the main purpose of Y6 homework was to prepare pupils for secondary school routines. Those secondary managers who felt that purposes changed somewhat with age stressed the particular demands of KS4 course work and GCSE preparation.

What seems to be emerging is that schools have defined a large number of purposes for homework, with priorities shifting mainly in relation to age and stage. The shift in priorities is mainly related to the relative roles of parent and child at each stage, and in the range of tasks which the child is expected to undertake 'independently' as he or she gets older.

One reason for encouraging a debate about the meaning and purpose of homework, as schools themselves have found, is that it is too easy to assume that definitions and purposes are shared, with possibly misleading implications. Do teachers and parents share an understanding about what parental involvement means, and how this may change as children get older? Is parental involvement being seen as an end rather than a means? If homework is intended to develop pupils' ability to work independently, what is being done to foster this? Are there important but implicit purposes for the homework programme - for example, to demonstrate to parents the commitment of the school to high standards?

One way of encouraging more active discussion would be for schools, parents or other groups to develop their own 'map' of the purposes which have been emphasised in this study, and in other studies reviewed in Appendix B. The aim of such an exercise would be to enable planners at any level to decide which purposes, if any are universal, and which are mainly relevant for some age groups or contexts. For example, a school might identify three key purposes, not all of which may be explicit in official documents:

- Raising achievement

- Improving home-school links

- Enhancing the reputation of the school

Raising achievement and home-school partnership would be found in almost all lists, but the strategies for achieving these goals might receive differing emphasis, depending on the school context. The third - enhancing the reputation of the school - is an often implicit, but significant purpose, certainly for senior managers. From each of these purposes it would be possible to derive a large number of more specific objectives, and this is where the differences between sub-groups could be identified and discussed.

Several of the schools we visited explained how purposes had been clarified through consultation, and how these were being worked out in practice in line with their long-term targets, as set out in the School Development Plan. But getting agreement about the purpose of homework could

not be achieved in isolation. It was part of a wider debate about the status of homework and its place within the broader school strategy.

1.3 The Status of Homework

One of the issues that has emerged from this discussion of the perceived purpose of homework is its status: how important do schools consider homework, and just why is it important? Is homework a useful extra, or an integral and essential part of the learning programme? If it is essential, does it follow that it is an entitlement? Is this the same as making it compulsory?

Almost all school policies and guidelines which we saw stressed the importance of homework and the contribution it makes to enhancing achievement. Some other indicators are therefore needed to assess how schools apply this principle in their practice. These indicators relate to the school's **expectations** about homework and its **integration** into the learning strategy.

Setting expectations

The indicators needed here are about **access** and **compliance.** If homework is to have high status, then it is essential that all pupils are enabled and required to complete it effectively. In other words, they all need access to the appropriate materials and conditions, which will vary according to the age, ability, special needs and home circumstances of the pupils. Once this challenge has been addressed, schools can be rigorous in applying rules about when and how the work should be completed. Some of the case study schools showed how these ideas could be put into practice, in ways which will be discussed in more detail in later chapters.

Ensuring access took a number of forms. For example, some primary schools felt that one of the best ways of helping pupils to manage their homework effectively was to put a major effort into strategies for enabling all parents to support and work with their children (see Chapter 2); this included, for example, providing guidelines and workshops on reading, spelling and writing, and ensuring all children had the basic materials. Every effort was made to encourage dialogue, not only between parent and teacher, but also between pupil and teacher (including in one school a confidential book, for noting difficulties the pupil did not want to air out loud in the classroom). Many primary schools were particularly concerned to ensure that pupils could succeed in their homework. Differentiation was tackled through tasks set at different levels or with different materials or goals. Extra support was offered in school by the Special Educational Needs co-ordinators (SENCOs), with special IT and other equipment for some pupils. Secondary schools seemed to find it harder to set differentiated homework tasks, but put considerable effort into offering support, with subject staff, learning support staff and mentors all ready to assist pupils during or after the school day (see 3.4). One school provided details of a community-based project to provide homework clubs for Asian girls. Teaching study skills was another way of equipping all pupils to tackle independent learning more effectively. Providing sufficient resources, particularly books, was often mentioned as a problem, although the telephone survey suggested that in general schools could supply what was needed; perhaps another interpretation is that homework tasks were designed to fit the available resources. However, problems persisted, with some schools unaware of how many pupils faced difficulties at home, without books, support or space for homework, or of the time some of them spent on extended tasks.

Then there was the issue of compliance. If homework is to be accepted as important by staff, pupils and parents, the school has to make the ground rules clear, apply them clearly and consistently and see they are respected (see 3.4). This proved more difficult in those primary schools which defined homework as a valuable but essentially voluntary activity, or left it to class teachers to decide the rules. Parents in particular appreciated clear, easily understood requirements about deadlines and requirements, and many primary schools provided these, often concentrating on the tasks and the schedule (when homework would be set and handed in or tested), rather than strict time allocations. These schedules often included short-term tasks, to be completed over a few days, and (for older pupils) occasional longer tasks, scheduled to last several weeks. More contentious was the question of sanctions; many

schools preferred monitoring and persuasion to punishment, being unwilling to put pupils off homework. In secondary schools, however, disciplinary procedures to ensure homework was completed and to deal with breaches were often rigorous and complex. Many schools made the requirements clear and explicit, often recording them in student planners. However, there was some in-built tension between the apparent clarity of the homework timetable, with time allocations and schedules set out for each subject, and the advice that departments retained some flexibility about when homework would be set.

Integrating homework into the learning programme

It was an accepted principle, to which most schools with written policies subscribed, that homework should be fully integrated into the learning programme, and that staff should not set 'one-off' tasks unrelated to the work in hand simply in order to satisfy the homework timetable. In what ways could this idea be demonstrated in practice? The three key ideas here concern **assessment**, **planning** and **evaluation.**

The school's view of the status of homework may show up in how it is **assessed** (see also 2.4). For example, some primary schools graded homework partly to show it was important and must be done, while others assessed it equally with class work as part of the formal programme to demonstrate that it was indeed integral. In the telephone survey, just over half the primary schools (51%) said that one of the strategies they encouraged staff to use to ensure that homework was completed was to make homework an essential part of pupils' assessed work. (By contrast some refused to assess work done at home because the standard was lower than class work, or parents had intervened too much). Others, particularly first schools, felt high status for homework was quite compatible with a more informal approach, especially on assessment. There were other ways than formal grades of rewarding good quality homework and underlining its importance. In both phases these included merit schemes and some form of public recognition or presentation. But the marking of homework was a contentious issue in many of the secondary schools we visited. Without clear guidance, it produced a burden of work for conscientious teachers which often resulted in slow and therefore less effective feedback to pupils. This could reduce the status and value of homework in the eyes of pupils. One school insisted that work should be returned at the next lesson after it had been handed in, but rapid turn-round sometimes meant marking was not as careful as the policy intended it to be. Other schools or departments suggested strategies for rigorous but selective assessment, to ensure that the results helped pupils to make progress in the classroom.

Guidance on **planning** homework and more especially on **evaluating** its quality also helped to indicate how seriously homework was taken by schools as a key element of their learning policy. Schools could demonstrate their commitment to integrating homework into the curriculum by making clear that homework had to be explicitly linked to the scheme of work and indicating how that might be done (see 2.1). In some cases, this meant planning in advance a set of homework tasks to complement class work for each module or topic, for example for a Year 7 art programme . In some primary schools staff had a two-pronged approach, with regular tasks such as spelling and tables fitting into the long-term strategy for literacy and numeracy, while year teams planned other tasks into their fortnightly outlines. In secondaries, subject departments had the responsibility for translating the principle of integration into practice, but it was actually quite unusual to find departmental systems for planning homework into schemes of work, with this task often being left to class teachers. Equally, only a few schools or departments had systematic procedures for evaluating the quality and effectiveness of homework tasks, and their contribution to the overall learning programme.

1.4 Overview: Scope, Purpose and Status of Homework

In this chapter we have shown that the meaning and purpose of homework are not always made explicit, and that there may be differing interpretations, between and within schools. To some extent this is because the nature of homework tasks, and the purposes they serve,

change and develop as children get older. There are also some indications that senior managers tend to see homework as serving a strategic purpose while other teachers may stress more pragmatic goals, such as expanding the time available for learning or allowing slower learners to catch up with the rest. Moreover, schools had not apparently always clarified or discussed their definition of homework, so that it was not clear (for example) whether it had to be *unaided* work, work done *at home* or a task that was *distinguishable from (though linked to) class work*. There was greater consensus in schools which had taken the trouble to discuss these issues as a staff, and to consult parents and others.

The status of homework in the school was indicated by the seriousness with which the school communicated and enforced its policy, and the practical strategies for realising the goal of integrating homework into the learning programme. This meant ensuring all pupils were given and enabled to complete relevant and appropriate homework, that every effort was made to see that they did it and that their work was valued through the quality of teachers' response to it.

It has become clear that the scope, purpose and status of homework programmes and policies depend on the contribution they make to broader school goals and strategies. We have looked briefly at the idea of homework as an integral part of an effective learning strategy. But this is not the only context. Homework may also be presented as part of one or more of the following:

- **a wider home/school policy**, including home-school contracts, communication with parents, parental support;

- **programmes to promote key skills** including supported self-study, individual action planning, independent learning;

- **strategies to promote community links**, including mentoring, links with libraries, parent and community groups/study centres.

More effective schools show how homework will contribute to the overall strategy to raise achievement, through these or other channels, rather than presenting homework almost as an end in itself.

Homework is a unique aspect of school policy

because it so clearly bestrides the dividing line between home and school. It therefore requires the active involvement of both pupils and parents, collaborating with school staff. Schools seem to have a better chance of achieving this involvement if their staff are clear and united on how homework can contribute positively to the broader goals of the school, particularly for more effective learning.

Such a holistic approach was clearly evident in the documents from one comprehensive school in the telephone survey, with an established programme for raising attainment through more effective learning and the involvement of all pupils, teaching and non-teaching staff and parents in this campaign. The homework policy was comprehensive, setting homework within the broader mission of the school, and all the parent/pupil leaflets carried the same message from 'Improving Secondary Schools' (Hargreaves, 1984), that five years of homework effectively adds one year of full-time education. But perhaps the most convincing evidence appears when homework has become part of the ethos of the school, as demonstrated by its practice, - as it clearly had in a primary school we visited (see Box 1.2).

In Chapter 2 we shall investigate in more detail how schools are using homework to enhance learning, in a wide variety of settings, focusing on the quality of their homework programme.

BOX 1.2
HOMEWORK AT THE HEART OF LEARNING

At this small rural primary school in a settled community, homework was very much part of the ethos of the school and had been an established part of life for many years. It was only when they wrote it down as a homework policy that they realised how much they were doing. There was a regular programme of literacy tasks (reading, spelling and book reviews) which were written into the English policy. Homework on topics were identified in short-term plans which were developed as a staff team. There was a clear timetable for all classes (for example Wednesday was spelling day). Tasks increased in depth and breadth (and time allocated) as pupils moved up the school. All homework was marked, in ways appropriate to the task. The same marking system was used for homework as for other work and occasionally (perhaps twice a term) homework was used to assign National Curriculum levels. Feedback was swift - KS1 pupils' work was marked with them, in KS2, work was returned the next day; corrections were required. Pupils enjoyed stimulating tasks and care was taken in matching work to children's ability. In fact, staff felt that homework had raised awareness of the needs of SEN pupils, which they did their best to meet. Parents felt they were kept well informed about what was expected, which helped them to plan. Pupils were also clear on what they had to do and why, and most agreed it helped them to achieve. As the headteacher commented, 'The world is a competitive place and I think homework gives them the edge'.

Indicators of Good Practice

1. **Scope.** LEAs and schools consult with staff, pupils, parents and relevant community groups in order to produce an agreed definition of what should count as homework.

2. **Purpose.** Similarly, the purposes of homework are made explicit and agreed by staff and parent representatives, and clear guidelines are drawn up in language appropriate for each group: staff, parents, pupils. If priorities differ for different age groups, this is made clear.

3. **Policy.** There is a homework policy which is clearly and explicitly related to the overall aims of the school, as outlined in the School Development Plan and other documents.

4. **Communication.** In addition to written guidelines and letters, schools are experimenting with other ways of clarifying the scope and purpose of homework, for example through in-service training, workshops for parents, tutorial sessions and opinion surveys.

2 Homework and Effective Learning: Forging the Link

This chapter moves from purpose to practice and addresses the key issue of effectiveness: how can schools ensure that homework is making a real contribution to effective learning? This requires action at all levels of management, from the head to classroom teacher, so that homework tasks fit the intended purpose and feed back into learning. The issues therefore relate mainly to the nature and **quality** of homework, rather than **quantity** (in terms of time allocations). We have separated these two aspects deliberately, partly because teachers we spoke to, particularly teachers in primary schools, insisted that it was the quality of the homework programme and the work it generated that was of prime importance. It is also true that the survey and visits were all targeted at schools which were committed to homework, usually for all their pupils. Questions about just how much time should be spent therefore seemed less important than the type of work that was to be done, and could be seen as part of the management agenda which will be considered in Chapter 3. Here the focus is on the learning agenda. We therefore look first at the range of homework tasks and objectives which schools appeared to be promoting (2.1) and then consider three general aspects of the teacher's strategy: planning homework tasks (2.2), matching them to pupils' capabilities (2.3) and assessing the outcomes (2.4). These principles are then applied to two key areas of primary school learning: English (language) and mathematics (2.5). The chapter ends with a short overview (2.6).

2.1 The Range of Tasks and Approaches

Homework tasks

What kinds of task were teachers setting for homework, and how did this change as pupils got older? In Chapter 2 we shall discuss answers to this question from several angles, but we start with a résumé of the evidence from the telephone survey. It should be remembered that this was supplied by the headteacher or another senior manager, who in larger schools might have little or no current teaching responsibility. In each case the interviewer was asked to say whether specific types of task, as listed in Table 2.1, were set regularly, often, occasionally or never.

Of the tasks listed, the most common (that is, those most likely to be set regularly) in the primary years were reading and written work; by KS3, written work was the most common. Over 40% of schools in both phases regularly set learning or revision tasks, a proportion which rose to 63% by Year 10. By that stage 'finding out information' had also become a regular activity in half the schools. Designing and making remained occasional tasks in most primary schools, but were apparently more common in KS3 and KS4. Finally, note that few senior managers considered that 'finishing off' class work was a regular occurrence (although 30% said it 'often' happened in Year 8 and 23% reported this for Year 10). Of course, such statistics only give the a bald indication of what was being done and no indication of whether the work was appropriate. But it confirms the impression from other studies and from our own school visits that, at least from KS2 onwards, there seemed to be a heavy emphasis on written tasks.

Table 2.1
Percentage of Schools Setting Tasks 'Regularly', by Year Group

Homework tasks	Y3 % of schools	Y6 % of schools	Y8 % of schools	Y10 % of schools
Reading	88	88	49	48
Written work	53	71	na	na
Written assignments	na	na	71	82
Written exercises	na	na	50	64
Learning/revising	44	46	42	63
Finding out information	25	34	37	51
Finishing off	10	12	16	13
Design/make	0	2	21	21
N=	225	198	141	141

All schools with the relevant year group
A series of single response items
na= not asked

Source: Diagnostics Telephone Survey of Primary and Secondary Schools, Oct. 1997

Table 2.2
Frequency of Homework Tasks: All pupils

Types of task done this term		Every week %	Sometimes %	Hardly ever %	Never %	No response %
Learning**	KS2	82	12	2	1	1
	KS3	40	46	12	2	1
Number work**	KS2	48	37	7	5	3
	KS3	66	30	3	1	1
Drawing**	KS2	16	55	18	8	3
	KS3	49	46	4	1	1
Writing*	KS2	22	52	18	5	2
	KS3	31	47	17	5	1
Finishing off**	KS2	19	36	23	18	4
	KS3	39	45	13	1	2
Research**	KS2	10	56	19	12	4
	KS3	7	73	14	5	1
Watching/ listening**	KS2	10	22	22	41	5
	KS3	6	15	39	39	2
Making things**	KS2	5	33	25	32	4
	KS3	6	25	36	31	2
Filling in worksheets (KS3 only)		22	47	24	5	1

N=1003

A series of single response items
Due to rounding errors, percentages may not always sum to 100
A total of 999 respondents answered at least one item in this question
*Statistically differences between KS2 and KS3 pupils: * $p= <.05$*
*** $p=<.001$*

Source: OFSTED KS2/KS3 Pupil Survey, Autumn 1997

In the case study schools, groups of pupils from KS2 and KS3 completed a questionnaire which included a list of homework tasks. They were asked to say which tasks they had done for homework this term. Their responses are summarised in Table 2.2.

It is important to present the results for the two phases separately because, as Table 2.2 shows, there was a significant difference for every item. This showed up most strongly in the tasks each group reported doing 'each week'. Of the items shown, 'learning' was by far the commonest for KS2 pupils, with over 80% seeing this as at least a weekly task (only about 40% of teachers said they set learning tasks 'regularly' for this age group). Both groups stressed 'number work, although KS3 pupils were more likely to do this each week. In fact, in the light of the TIMSS study (Keys et al., 1997a,b) in which 96% of pupils of this age reported doing maths homework the percentages for both KS2 and KS3 pupils seem low; perhaps because in our survey they were asked about number work ('doing sums or problems'). The secondary pupils were also more likely than those in primary school to report 'drawing' tasks, suggesting that these featured in a number of subjects; and also 'finishing off', with almost 40% of KS3 pupils saying they did this each week (rather higher than the teacher reports from the telephone survey would suggest). Indeed, KS3 pupils reported a wider range of weekly tasks than KS2; other than learning and number work, less than a quarter of the KS2 pupils said they did any of the other tasks 'every week'. The contrast was less marked for 'writing', and indeed it is perhaps surprising that less than a third said they had writing tasks each week; this may suggest that 'writing' was taken to mean 'creative writing' rather than written exercises. The last two activities on the list (watching/listening and making things) were uncommon for either group; well over half hardly ever or never did them. The change in the pattern of some homework tasks as pupils got older also applied within key stages. Weekly number work increased steadily each year from Year 5 (45%) to Year 8 (68%); 'drawing' tasks also became more common over each year over the same age range, as did 'finishing off' (48% of Year 8 reported this as a weekly occurrence).

One small indicator that teachers themselves recognised that 'finishing off' happened more often than they would have wished came from the telephone survey. When primary head teachers and secondary senior managers were asked about the types of task set for homework, well under a fifth of each group reported the regular use of 'finishing off'. However, when primary head-teachers with their own class were asked about the homework tasks they had actually set in the previous week, considerably more of that group (39%) had used this option.

While the teacher and pupil data cannot be directly compared, since it came from different sets of schools and the questions differed in several respects, the evidence raises questions about the range of intended and actual activities. To what extent do teachers, individually or collectively, aim to provide a varied diet of tasks, or to develop the type of activity as children get older and more competent? How good is the fit between the school's policy on homework tasks appropriate to each key stage and the activities actually set for classes each week?

Dimensions of homework

Another way of analysing the types of work teachers set for homework was by asking those we met in schools to review the way they integrated homework with classroom learning analytically. We asked them to consider a number of 'dimensions' relating to the purpose of homework within the overall learning strategy, and to discuss where their practice fitted on each of them. (Figure 2.1). While the diagram showed contrasting goals on each dimension, we expected that many teachers would consider both to be relevant, for some groups or some purposes, and this indeed was the case, but these discussions showed up certain patterns and enabled teachers to identify priorities. In practice, several of the dimensions overlapped and we shall select three here in order to pick up some key findings.

Written work versus other modes. This dimension picks up the issue identified by the survey, namely the apparent predominance (in teacher reports) of written work, especially from KS2 onwards. In KS1, written work was not a major component. Indeed one first school said that no written work was set as homework, although this was not the case for KS1 generally. Some **primaries** stressed that much of the writing was informal - making notes and lists - or was an integral part of tasks demanding a number of modes, including reading, interviewing, model-making and drawing:

➡ At a semi-rural primary school with 123 pupils, all the KS2 pupils were undertaking a project on the Victorians during the autumn term. While the two younger classes each had a history homework assignment appropriate to their age group, the top class (Years 5 and 6) had three assignments linked directly to the topic: on Victorian toys and games, the Great Exhibition and a 'Victorian Christmas party'. All involved inquiry, reading, creativity, planning and presentation, in a variety of modes.

One school suggested that, even in English, homework was more to do with preparation for writing, which would usually be done in class - to ensure quality; although another school said that 'writing up in best' was done as homework. A concern expressed about extended written work at home was whether parents would intervene too much; but schools with strong parental links felt this was not an issue, if the appropriate explanation had been given and both pupils and parents were clear about how the task should be tackled. Schools which had planned their homework programme with progression in mind stressed that written work had to be set in context and developed gradually, so that the writing was based on careful preparation and reading, always for a clear purpose and balanced by other modes of recording where appropriate. These principles also applied to mathematics, where practical and investigative work was often seen as very appropriate for homework, from the earliest years. In several primary schools, written work was much more frequent in Years 5 and 6, with regular and sometimes quite lengthy written assignments being set. Since many schools stressed that a key purpose for homework was to prepare pupils for secondary school, it needs to be asked whether these assignments were more of a response to the perceived demands of secondary school homework than a natural extension to the KS2 learning

Figure 2.1
'Dimensions of Homework' Sheet

DIMENSIONS OF HOMEWORK		
Completion Finishing off class work, 'catching up', following up what has been done in class	*versus*	**Preparation** Reading around new unit/text, research for project, learning new terms
Reinforcement Practice exercises, learning, revising	*versus*	**Research** Information retrieval, from school or home sources
Written work Essays, notes, compositions, exercises, diagrams	*versus*	**Other modes** Reading, oral inquiry, practical work, drawing, painting
Time-limited E.g. exercise timed to last 20 mins; set of 10 'spellings'.	*versus*	**Open-ended** E.g. 'Research' task, TV review, practical design
Direct parent involvement E.g. parent reading with/to child	*versus*	**Pupil independence encouraged** E.g. Year 6 pupils, preparing for secondary, parental encouragement only
School resources only Homework can be completed with textbook or other school-supplied materials only	*versus*	**Non-school resources important** Pupils encouraged/expected to use library, home, family members' experience
'Overnight' task Short-term task to be completed in one homework session	*versus*	**Longer-term task** Homework used to contribute to progress of ongoing topic

programme. This issue seems an important one to address in cross-phase discussions.

Visits to **secondary** schools produced evidence in line with the findings of the telephone survey, in suggesting that by KS3 written tasks predominated in homework. Some English departments insisted that one of the two assignments each week should be something other than written work (usually reading), as much to lessen the burden of marking as for pedagogical reasons. There were examples of other modes being used in KS3, for example in art or technology assignments, or in the learning required in foreign languages; and later as pupils moved to KS4 and embarked on the research and preparation for GCSE course work. Visits suggested that in practice it was relatively unusual for schools or departments to suggest or specify the range of homework activities that might be appropriate. For example, one school's policy recommended that staff should employ a variety of activities, including: investigations, research, interviews, drafting, report writing, simple experiments, projects, model-making, reading, revising, visiting the public library, word-processing. Even when this was stated, it could be difficult to ensure that the policy was consistently

implemented, although it seems that in this case the range of tasks set for KS3 pupils was indeed more varied than usual.

Reinforcement/consolidation *versus* research/open-ended. All primary schools stressed the importance of using homework to reinforce learning, through reading and handwriting practice, and learning spellings, mathematics facts and number patterns. These were seen to be important throughout the primary years but in many schools formed the bulk of homework tasks in KS1, with 'research' - information seeking and preparatory work of many kinds - becoming more prominent in KS2. A number of schools stressed the importance of reinforcement activities for pupils with special needs, although here too they aimed for balance, with a chance for pupils to take part in investigations and inquiry. 'Research' activities could take many forms, and be made appropriate for most age groups:

➡ At a London primary, Year 2 children were asked to find out for homework why leaves fall off trees in autumn. Two sample responses were provided, one which described but did not explain the process, the other with a good attempt at explanation:

Leaves fall off the tree because they are very weak. They fall in Autumn, because the leaves get very dry and they can crunch so that means the wind can easily blow them off the branches on the tree...

➡ At a GM primary Year 5 pupils were asked to apply what they had learned in class about data-bases by drawing up a simple database of their own. One girl produced two examples: a family chart, showing the name, age, height, weight and hair colour of each family member; and another listing weights (imperial and metric) of a variety of foods.

It is interesting that secondary schools reported a similar evolution from reinforcement to research, with homework developing more of a research focus in KS4 as an aspect of GCSE course work requirements. In other words, in each phase, reinforcement tasks were felt to be more appropriate for younger pupils, with research only being introduced later, rather than a steady progression in both types of task. Several reasons were put forward in secondary schools for the initial emphasis on reinforcement. Some departments, particularly English and mathematics, felt the need to reinforce core skills and knowledge during KS3, and others (especially foreign languages) were anxious to lay sound foundations in new areas of learning. There was then a renewed need for reinforcement in preparation for Year 9 assessment. There was also concern about standards of 'research'; one head of history had stopped setting such tasks for Year 7 because the bulk of what was presented was taken directly from common computer packages and he did not think this was of real benefit.

Direct parent involvement *versus* pupil independence encouraged. Many schools pointed out this dimension was very much a case of 'both and' rather than 'either or'. Some saw the gradual development of the child's ability to organise and manage his or her own work as one of the key indicators of progression in their homework programme. The transition from 'parent as teacher' to 'pupil as teacher' was actively encouraged, and could start in KS1. It was seen as a valuable educational exercise for pupils to explain their task to parents. There will be examples throughout Chapter 2 of ways in which parents were encouraged to collaborate over

homework, with the type of involvement changing as children got older. One instance of the transition could be seen in some reading records, where children as well as parents were encouraged to write their own comments. By Year 6, parents' main role had often changed to one of support and encouragement, sometimes for pragmatic reasons. As one teacher commented, '*Some Year 6 pupils have gone beyond their own parents' understanding*'. Indeed, some teachers pointed out the equal opportunities issue which could arise: as one said, '*tasks should not require parental involvement to recognise that some pupils do not get help at home*'. Continuing parental involvement was seen as crucial, however, for pupils with special needs (see 2.3 below).

Again, secondary schools mirrored their primary counterparts in expecting a gradual decrease in parental involvement and corresponding increase in pupil independence from 11 to 16. A recurrent issue was what kind of contribution schools looked for beyond co-operation in seeing that homework was completed. In other words, do secondary schools expect or want parents to assist in any way with the work pupils do at home? Guidelines and information for parents suggested that this would be welcome, and one school reported that when particularly difficult or unusual pieces of work were set for Year 7 pupils there were large numbers of letters to the head of year and many more comments by parents in homework diaries. However, as we shall see in Chapters 3 and 4, parents sometimes felt the school had not made their role clear, particularly as their children got older - perhaps from Year 6 onwards. What was fair or unfair help? What if teachers had not made the task clear, or supplied the necessary resources? What if the child had not yet acquired the study skills to work independently? These questions seemed to arise more often in secondary schools, with a pupil's homework being set by many teachers who might have differing expectations.

For the school, it was important to balance the parental role with responsibility to the pupil. Developing the pupil's ability to work independently was, after all, often seen as an important purpose for homework. The better these skills were developed, the less dependent pupils would be on parents; and it had to be recognised, some teachers felt, that some parents seemed unwilling or unable to help, or else were over-protective. One recurring dilemma for many schools, we shall find, was how they could most effectively harness 'parent power' to achieve the goals of their homework programme, while at the same time meeting the needs of all pupils, whatever their family background.

There were examples of schools teaching skills for independent learning progressively, through the type and amount of structuring given for a homework task. There were also study skill modules, often as part of KS3 tutorial programmes. It was less common to find a coherent strategy for planning or evaluating the changing role of parents and children in carrying out homework. However, this was just one aspect of the larger issue of how homework is planned, where we found practice varied widely, especially between primary and secondary schools.

2.2   Planning

Do teachers plan their homework with as much care as they take in designing their schemes of work? Indeed, how do they plan homework to complement the classroom programme? Policies suggest that homework should always be set for a purpose that is integral to learning. But in working to this end, some teachers perceive a tension between pre-planning (e.g. building a bank of homework assignments explicitly linked to modules or topics) and flexibility (e.g. ensuring homework arises out of and is relevant to the way each teacher is working with each class). This may overlap with a tension between planning which is managed by a subject leader and the professional autonomy which a class teacher may feel is the foundation of effective teaching.

We shall look first at the way teachers planned their homework programmes, first in terms of broad **frameworks** for skill development across age groups (and perhaps across the curriculum), then for assignments linked to **curriculum content,** and lastly at how these plans were shared with **pupils and parents**. This will lead to a review of the benefits and costs of systematic homework planning.

Creating general frameworks

In primaries, there tends to be a division between core homework tasks intended to reinforce classroom learning, such as reading, spelling and tables, which may follow a whole-school plan or scheme, and 'topic' tasks, which are often devised by the year group team or class teacher, within the general topic framework. Nevertheless, there were differences in the general approach to planning homework in the primary schools we visited. Some schools had devised a very clear framework which catered for progression and differentiation in literacy and numeracy, could be readily understood and followed by parents and pupils and also allowed teachers some flexibility in planning it into their classroom programme. For example:

➡ At a small rural primary, the staff had made book reviews the backbone of their KS2 language homework programme. Using a variety of published and home-produced guidelines, pupils gradually learned how to develop a critique. With guidance, pupils in Years 3 and 4 chose one book to review per month (two books for Years 5 and 6). The head had gone to considerable trouble to select appropriate materials and to bring in new books, including a particular genre for reluctant readers. Starting with a very structured approach, pupils could progress to really quite sophisticated reviews by Year 6. In addition, pupils had to prepare a talk on the book to give to the class. Other aspects of the framework included a spelling programme (from Year 2, based on a published scheme) with a clear weekly schedule, a scheme for tables and a reading programme for KS1.

➡ At a slightly larger primary the headteacher had introduced a whole-school systematic approach to homework which involved a structured programme for each class, from Reception onwards, worked out when the curriculum was planned for each term. The emphasis was on English and mathematics, with the whole school following the same structured spelling programme. All KS1 children were expected to take a 'Spot' book home each night - that is, a free choice story book classified for reading level, not their reading scheme book. Mathematics homework started with learning number bonds, mathematics facts and tables, with KS2 pupils also having a mathematics investigation each week. All the requirements were very clearly set out in the Homework Policy, and in letters to the parents of each class.

➡ At a primary school in outer London the subject co-ordinators for English and mathematics had each worked out a homework programme in their subject area for all year groups. The emphasis was on basic skills two or three times per week. Typical homework for Year 3 would include reading, spelling, grammar (e.g. punctuation) and mathematics exercises, as well as learning tables. Specific days were designated for reading with parents. Within this framework, class teachers could plan their own activities.

The idea of establishing a clear framework for homework tasks which reinforce literacy and numeracy was found both in junior schools and first schools, urban and rural schools and was usually linked to a clear lead by the headteacher. In one London primary the direction was clearly set from the top, and all prospective teachers were told about the homework programme at interview. The headteacher saw all plans written by class teachers, and homework was identified in both half-term and weekly planning, the main emphasis being on the revision of basic skills. In a rural junior school there was a whole-school agreement that English and mathematics allocations should be written into the subject policies and a structure of regular core tasks was laid down, with time allocations, for reading, spelling and tables. One approach to defining the framework was to choose a common scheme for the whole school or key stage. In one school a published mathematics scheme and reading scheme had been chosen partly because they had in-built homework activities.

In secondary schools there were few equivalents to these whole-school programmes of regular core homework tasks. First of all, all homework was planned within subject departments and, secondly, for all except the youngest pupils or those with special needs whose basic skills needed to be reinforced, there was a pressure to use homework mainly to press forward with curriculum coverage. Within subjects, particularly in foreign languages

and to some extent in English and mathematics, teachers were sometimes encouraged to plan regular reinforcement tasks - for example, learning vocabulary or working through a booklet on grammar and the use of written language. More often, however, homework was linked directly to the content of specific classroom units or themes, and in both phases planning these topic or subject assignments had to be approached rather differently from the general framework for skill development.

Planning for content-linked topics, themes or units

How did schools plan content-linked homework assignments? In primary schools this depended to some extent on their general approach to curriculum planning. Staff who planned in teams, whether for the medium or shorter term, often wrote the homework task into the plan, at least in outline, at the same time. Sometimes these outlines were made more specific in short-term plans:

➡ At a grant maintained one-form-entry primary school the staff produced a curriculum map, which was sent out to parents each term, outlining in general terms the homework that KS2 pupils would be expected to cover. They also wrote a specific homework task onto the curriculum planning sheet for each two-week unit. Thus Year 4 children would be expected to *design and make a parachute to support a Lego brick, and draw and label the design* as the homework for a science unit on friction and air resistance. This would be in addition to the regular programme of reading, spelling and learning tables, which had started in KS1.

➡ At a first school homework was derived from class work and seen as an extension of it. As such, it was written into one, two or three-week units of work. These assignments included investigative work in mathematics and science.

➡ At a village primary, planning of topic-related tasks had been taken much further and was fully integrated into termly plans. Class Three (Years 2 and 3), taught on a job-share by two teachers, had a clear list of the five tasks which were set for the term, in addition to the routine homework programme. These tasks were set every two weeks and each had a different subject focus, related to the term's topics (see Figure 2.2). A similar list of tasks was prepared for the older pupils, this time with guidelines for the pupils included on each assignment.

In secondary schools, this kind of detailed pre-planning of homework for a unit or a term's work, for one class or for a whole year group, seemed to be much less common until it was needed for GCSE course work. However, some KS3 examples were found in the schools we visited.

➡ One 11-18 comprehensive school in a northern city had examples of careful departmental planning in science, history and art for Year 7 pupils. Booklets had been prepared for a term's work in science, providing each pupil with a set of self-contained assignments related to the unit on electricity they were studying. A special version had been prepared for pupils with learning difficulties, who completed some of the homework topics on a longer time scale. In the same school, the art department had set the pace for the design faculty in the standard of the project booklets (which again incorporated homework tasks) as well as in the guidance to pupils on assessment and other design teams were taking up the approach.

➡ Staff at a boys' comprehensive school had written homework tasks into the scheme of work in English and developed a bank of science homework assignments which teachers were encouraged to use.

➡ The mathematics department in a grant-maintained grammar school had developed a collection of homework sheets which could be used to reinforce class work.

However, in most of the secondary schools we visited, and in most departments, homework was not systematically included in the advance planning of schemes of work or subject modules undertaken by many teaching teams for their classroom programmes. Some schools expressed the view that it would be inappropriate to write homework tasks into teaching schemes, because it was part of the teacher's professional responsibility to devise homework assignments that would meet the specific learning needs of his or her class. But as we have seen, other departments felt that advance planning and preparation could enable teachers to

Figure 2.2
Class Three's Homework Topic Tasks

[extract from letter to parents]
Other homework tasks have a two-week time limit which is clearly written on the paper which comes home. There will be five tasks this term...

Class 3 Autumn term 1997

Homework Tasks

1. *Set on 26/9/97 To be given in by 10/10/97* Science/Art focus. Draw, in pencil, the front view of your home.

2. *Set on 24/10/97. To be given in by 7/11/97* English/History focus. Write a report of your visit to Wimpole Hall

3. *Set on 7/11/97. To be given in by 21/11/97.* Geography focus. Activity sheet reinforcing work done in class on compass points

4. *Set on 21/11/97. To be given in by 5/12/97.* English focus. Write a rhyme to go in a Christmas card. (Formula provided if needed.)

5. *Set on 5/12/97. To be given in by 16/12/97.* RE focus. Write, and/or draw, to tell/show me how you celebrate Christmas in your home

meet those needs more easily and effectively, with no loss of autonomy. The issue here is whether some advance planning of homework - for example, of a collection of resopurces, tasks or materials linked to schemes of work - is as relevant or professionally appropriate as advanced planning of classroom programmes. The evidence suggested many schools did not see it this way. Thus in an 11-18 GM comprehensive which had received complimentary comments on homework in its inspection report, the researcher found that few departmental schemes of work included detailed recommendations for suitable homework tasks. The English department had a very detailed scheme for each year group, linking particular thematic content to the development of particular skill areas, but it did not touch on homework tasks.

Planning with parents and pupils

We have seen that some schools felt that making homework assignments explicit would actually help teachers, pupils and parents to focus more effectively on the task. Planning homework for KS1 pupils, especially for the youngest groups, could often mean preparing materials which parents could use with their children, and in some cases introducing this through workshop sessions:

➡ A large first school (309 on roll) ran workshops for the parents of 'Rising Fives' to explain the school's approach to learning and to set out 'Targets for Home Practice'. Each area of the 'Targets' was discussed and examples of work in school were shown. As teachers explained, this information was personalised for each child, with individual targets added or subtracted. A list of methods for parents and teachers to co-operate was drawn up, including ideas for parents who could observe the teacher in school and mini-workshops for practical activities.

➡ Another first school, with a more informal approach to homework, had also taken trouble to prepare simple mathematical games which parents could use to reinforce basic concepts.

➡ A northern urban primary had prepared packs of activity sheets to reinforce the Key Word vocabulary through 'games' at home which required the parent to act as 'teacher' or at least facilitator.

Even in KS1, however, teachers were preparing pupils to take on more responsibility. This might involve careful planning, to ensure that the pupils really knew how to tackle a task. The last school mentioned above introduced 'personal studies' in KS2, and staff felt it was important to introduce the task in stages, working closely with pupils and their parents:

➡ For Year 4 pupils, a letter was sent home explaining the personal study and how it was linked to the term's history project on explorers. They had to choose a famous explorer and then prepare a written account of his life and significance as homework over one month. The pupils had been prepared for this task by the approach taken in class work within science, history and geography. By Year 6, pupils were carrying out one personal study a term, and two pages of detailed and fairly sophisticated guidelines were prepared for pupils, as well as a workshop for parents who were anxious about how (and how much) to help.

Similar care was taken, in the school which used book reviews as the core of its written work, in planning the work progressively with pupils as they became more skilled in their approach. In both cases, staff also had to prepare pupils for giving an oral presentation of their findings.

The benefits and costs of planning

Those who had made the commitment to careful pre-planning of homework programmes and assignments - mainly in primary schools - felt that the **benefits** were considerable. From the teachers' point of view, when the planning was done together, it helped them to look critically at issues of **continuity and progression**, in homework as much as in class work. They described how this had made them much more careful to ensure that children were being given appropriate challenges. This was particularly apparent with whole-school schemes for language and number work, but also applied to frameworks for developing study skills, in personal studies, science investigations or book reviews. It also promoted **consistency** of approach, particularly in the teaching of basic skills, which boosted the confidence of pupils and reassured parents, who knew what to expect and felt better equipped to support their children. Thirdly, it meant that less experienced teachers had a **clear framework** within which to work and even a bank of homework materials to draw on. Most importantly, **goals were made explicit**. This meant that teachers and others could see how far they were achieving their aim of integrating homework fully within the overall learning programme. For school managers in particular, explicit homework plans, however they were designed, meant that their relevance and feasibility could be readily monitored and evaluated.

There were also benefits for **parents and pupils**. To some extent, some of these were related to the management of the process, a theme we shall pursue in Chapter 3. For example, parents clearly appreciated knowing what was to be done and when, particularly for regular tasks. But many also liked to know about the topics coming up later in the term, and how they might be expected to help. The popularity of workshops and materials to help introduce four and five-year olds to written language and number concepts is a clear indication how many parents are ready and willing to co-operate with the school in their child's learning, as long as they are shown what to do. The termly letters to parents, and class newsletters - sometimes produced by the pupils - could also be used both to inform parents about homework assignments that were coming up and to involve them, if they wished, in the process. Most pupils also liked to know what was expected, and particularly appreciated clear advance planning for the topic assignments - almost universally preferred to routine tasks.

At secondary school it was more difficult to ascertain the benefits of systematically planned homework, especially for pupils, since it was relatively uncommon. The science department which had produced the homework booklets described above pointed out that the system provided parents with information on what was coming up and feedback on progress, since marks for each assignment were recorded on the front of the booklet. Certainly, comments from Year 7 pupils suggested that problems with homework often arose as a result of insufficient planning; for example, inadequate guidelines for extended written work, questions to answer without the relevant resources or several subject assignments arriving at once.

The **costs and challenges** of systematic planning were well recognised. The main cost was in staff time and energy, with an associated expenditure in reprographics for schemes that involved the production of materials and information sheets. However, some teachers, particularly in secondary schools, were worried that systematic advance planning would produce a rigid system that failed in its central purpose, of ensuring that homework was fully integrated with learning. They argued that even experienced teachers could not know in advance how a class would react to teaching materials, and therefore pre-planned assignments could prove inappropriate and inhibit teachers from using homework as they felt it should be used: to address aspects of class work which were proving particularly difficult, and to adapt the work to the capability of the class as a whole. An English department suggested that pre-planned assignments were inappropriate in a subject which worked on themes rather than units or modules of work. However, some departments felt they had overcome these problems by developing banks of assignments, broadly linked to themes or topics, which could be selected by teachers to meet the needs of each class.

The argument about planning versus flexibility could be seen most clearly in relation to SEN pupils and their work. Undoubtedly, such pupils would be penalised by any system which expected them to keep up with a set of pre-planned class assignments, and flexibility was needed in setting work appropriate for individuals. But SENCOs who were able to work closely with subject departments saw the answer in more careful planning, rather than a flexible, *ad hoc* approach (see 2.3 below).

There was undoubtedly a marked difference between primary and secondary schools in their approach to the issue of homework planning, with primary schools generally assuming that homework would be considered as part of the curriculum planning process and most secondary schools distinguishing more sharply between pre-planned classroom programmes and flexible homework assignments. While secondary specialists might see pre-planning of homework as neither necessary nor even helpful, there were also risks attached to a flexible approach. If this was not carefully managed, it could lead to the over-use or misuse of 'finishing off', reducing homework merely to an extension of time to complete class work tasks. As we indicated in Chapter 1, some schools saw the completion of assignments started as a perfectly legitimate form of homework, and explained how some teachers might introduce homework tasks during a lesson in order to be sure that pupils knew what to do. But this is very different from the fallback position taken by a teacher who has failed to meet his goals for a lesson with all or some pupils and tells them to 'finish it off' for homework. Perhaps what is needed is a more constructive debate about 'finishing off', to identify why it is generally not seen as an effective strategy by those who write policies, and yet persists in many classrooms.

2.3 Matching Homework to Pupils' Capabilities

It is a widely accepted principle that pupils should be set appropriate learning targets and that learning approaches and possibly materials should be differentiated to achieve this goal. Should this principle be applied to homework and, if so, how have schools approached the challenge? We shall look first at strategies for differentiating homework, for all pupils, and then more specifically at homework for children with special educational needs.

Differentiating homework

There is a close link between this issue and the preceding one, since most forms of differentiation require advance planning, related again to the specific task and the materials supplied to pupils to complete it. However, there were other approaches. One was to allow for 'differentiation by outcome'; that is, all pupils would be set the same task with the expectation that they would differ in the quality and quantity of their response. The other was to plan different tasks for groups who had already been differentiated by ability.

In the telephone survey, schools were asked whether they gave different homework allocations to pupils within the same class. Half the primary schools did so but only 17% of the secondary schools. Part of the reason for this was organisational. The visits to primary schools confirmed that the majority of primary teachers group their children by ability within the class for certain activities, usually in literacy and numeracy. Of those giving differing allocations, almost all (92%) said they used such ability groupings as a basis for differentiating homework tasks. But 'differentiation by outcome' was also common, since 90% of the same group also said they often set the same task but had differing expectations based on their knowledge of pupils.

In secondary schools, by contrast, any ability grouping is generally at year-group level, sorting pupils into sets or bands, rather than within the class. One London school, for example, streamed its boys by ability in Years 7 and 8 and organised them in ability sets from Year 9. In such schools, heads of department therefore felt that with the reduced range of ability in each class it was generally appropriate to devise a single task for the whole class, although the head of mathematics occasionally provided special tasks for individuals. Even in schools with mixed ability classes in KS3, however, it was common to set undifferentiated homework tasks, except perhaps for SEN pupils. The difficulties this could pose for pupils were recognised in the homework policy of a comprehensive school in the survey which had a long-standing programme to raise achievement through more effective learning for all pupils:

Homework tasks can be very demanding for some pupils. Make sure that resources are accessible, e.g. books are not always available at home and students need to have research skills (go through the methods with them).

Ideally, we should have differentiated homework tasks and although this is often difficult to organise it gives students the opportunity to achieve success independently.

In the primary schools we visited, it was common practice for teachers to differentiate the core homework tasks designed to reinforce classroom learning. Very often, the class was organised into three or four ability groups and this structure was used to assign both class work and homework. In schools with a well structured homework framework, this proved a straightforward task. All children might be expected to undertake the same task (learning spellings or tables) but the content would depend on their progress within the scheme.

➡ At a primary in inner London with 51% on free school meals, ability groups were used as the basis for defining homework. This could mean six or seven levels of spelling within the school's spelling scheme, with extension work for the most able.

➡ At a village school with some mixed age classes, Class Three worked in two groups, and homework tasks in core skills were planned for each. Sometimes the same task was set (for example on mathematical vocabulary), but learning tasks were differentiated. The planning sheet showed that when Group 1 were working on number bonds, Group 2 were practising their tables (2x, 5x, 3x) and when, later in the term, Group 1 were starting on 2x multiplication facts, Group 2 were completing a puzzle sheet using the 4x table.

This principle was sometimes extended to related tasks such as mathematical games or written assignments.

➡ At a primary school with an informal approach to homework, mathematics games were sent home regularly for Reception pupils on Tuesdays and Thursdays. These games included skills for matching, sorting and number recognition. Pupils would be given games appropriate to their understanding, to play with their parents - a system which the latter understood well.

➡ At a suburban primary school with a highly organised homework programme, more able pupils were generally given open-ended investigations, while for the less able the task was given more structure, with specific questions to answer.

Most schools designed their topic assignments so that they could be tackled by all pupils, with the inevitable differences in outcome, which could be considerable even in KS1, as the task on why leaves fall in autumn (pp24–25) indicated. By selecting a mode other than writing, such as drawing or listening/speaking, the teacher could enable pupils to express their ideas on a more equal footing, although care had to be taken that this was not just a substitute, to keep the child busy but unchallenged.

Schools provided a number of examples of pupils taking the initiative to extend their school learning voluntarily through extended work at home; for example a well-produced 'Dear Diary...' written over a half-term week, and inquiries sparked off by historical projects at school. Enthusiasm of this kind was most often found at the beginning of KS2. In addition, some primaries had arranged additional opportunities for some KS2 pupils to extend their written work. For example in a junior school the higher attainers in Years 5 and 6 were taken once a week by the headmaster, who set them formal written tasks:

Write an essay in 45 minutes to discuss what language is used for, and the different types of communication

In other schools, enrichment might take the form of extra activities for the whole class, such as taking part in a local competition to design a plaque for the local shopping centre.

Meeting special needs

All the schools we visited had made some attempt to adapt homework tasks for pupils with special needs. Many schools offered extra support to help pupils with SEN to complete their homework. But the key issue was how far the SENCO was able to work closely with teachers in selecting and designing tasks to meet pupils' needs. In general, there were two approaches which might well be combined. The first was for the SENCO to define specific learning targets for the individual, usually in literacy and/or numeracy, to write these in the Individual Education Plan (IEP) and to share them with the child's teacher(s) and if possible the parents. The second approach was for the SENCO to collaborate with the class or subject teacher in working through class material, in order to assess how tasks could be adapted, or the child supported in carrying out the same task as other pupils. In general, it seemed that only a minority of primary schools were able to use their SENCO in this second way; in the telephone survey, it seemed that less than 10% involved the SENCO in decisions about homework. However, the schools we visited provided examples of the valuable contribution which the SENCO could make.

➡ In a primary in the north east, the SENCO worked with KS1 teachers on early homework writing tasks and referred teachers to resources that would help them to match work to the needs of pupils with special needs; for example high interest books for older pupils experiencing difficulties with reading.

➡ In a rural first school with 300 pupils, the head teacher acted as SENCO, but in conjunction with a special needs team including another teacher and a classroom support assistant. Homework was planned according to the stage (of the SEN Code) the pupils were at. For pupils at Stage 1, where progress was being monitored by the class teacher, these pupils were given key word games to take home and play to develop their retention of these words. Pupils at Stage 2 added to this task homework specifically linked to their IEP targets. There was a space on the IEP sheet for 'home contributions' and reinforcement with parental involvement was felt to be the main aspect of homework. There was a strong belief in 'overlearning' for pupils with SEN; this was considered to be effective in helping them to make progress and depended on regular parental support.

By contrast, in one London primary the SENCO worked in parallel rather than in collaboration with the class teacher. There, IEPs had four targets, two set by the class teacher and two by the SENCO, both of whom set homework. In some schools, the SENCO found all the designated time taken up with assessment and administration and had hardly any direct involvement in teaching or in helping with homework.

In secondary schools, there was the same distinction between schools where the special needs or learning support department actively collaborated with subject colleagues in helping to differentiate materials, including homework tasks, and those where their work was more strictly confined to support for individuals. Only two of the ten secondary schools visited provided clear examples of collaboration, on homework materials or the development of basic skills. One of these was a northern comprehensive with a mixed intake, with ability scores on entry below the national average:

➡ The SENCO worked closely with departments to encourage an emphasis on quality rather than quantity. The aim was to ensure that staff were made aware of the time element in setting homework for SEN pupils, whose work should be marked for effort. For example in mathematics, SEN pupils were not asked to 'do 50 worked examples' if fewer would achieve the same result. In English, there was an emphasis on the basics rather than extension work, but the SENCO found it difficult to evaluate the effectiveness of this approach. SEN pupils were aware that they received less homework than other pupils in terms of quantity, but it was supposed to be just as regular and to meet high standards. The major problem for SEN pupils was irregularity of attendance - they were often not there when the homework was set.

This example raises several of the issues which schools found difficult in making homework 'fair' for all pupils. Should fairness be defined in terms of inputs (all given the same task) or outcomes (all required to expend the same effort)? Should those who worked faster be given additional or more challenging work - or those who worked slowly be given less?

Some SENCOs felt strongly about this:

➡ One SENCO in a GM comprehensive school felt subject teachers had not thought about this sufficiently, with the result that some SEN pupils were becoming very distressed at their inability to do the work set. They could not structure or complete the heavy burden of written tasks. As a result, they often relied heavily on parents and older siblings to help them complete homework in order to avoid

penalties. With no framework for collaboration with subject staff, the special needs staff had set up a SEN homework club every lunchtime.

The very real difficulties that could arise for pupils with SEN were well illustrated in memos from the SENCO sent in by one of the survey schools (Figure 2.4). Note that these memos were sent only a few weeks into the autumn term, suggesting that these Year 7 pupils were having an unhappy introduction to homework in their new school. There was another about a Year 10 pupil, suggesting that problems could persist.

Figure 2.4
Problems with Homework for Year 7 Pupils with SEN

Memo

To: All staff who teach M......, 7C
From: [SENCO]
Date: 17.09.97

M... is becoming distressed at home with regard to homework. She ... does not portray all the usual features of a child with learning difficulties. However, she does worry terribly and is spending over three hours on homework on some days. Please try to differentiate homework. Her mother has been told to stop her after half an hour per subject, she will write a note in M...'s book when this happens.

If there are any problems please see me. Thanks.

Memo

To: All staff who teach A......, 7X
From: [SENCO]
Date: 17.09.97

A.. is becoming more and more distressed at home with regard to homework. This is becoming a major problem within the family and causing great upset. Please try to differentiate homework and classwork wherever possible. A... has been in a special school and has not had any homework before. She has a very short concentration span, 10 minutes perhaps maximum - this is improving on a daily basis. At the moment please can you give her a homework which may involve colouring a picture or finding a picture in a magazine or newspaper. If the class have five questions to answer allow her to find one, gradually building up the amount she has to do. Her tutor group are aware of her difficulties and slowly accepting her.

If A... gets distressed with her homework her parents will stop her, this may result in homework not being done, please accept this for the time being...

She has, however, done extremely well and responds to praise and merit marks. She has a target sheet (smiley faces) and this is filled in every day. She also has a home/school book, please feel free to use it to convey messages to her parents.

While ability differences were generally recognised as a possible ground for differentiating homework tasks, even if it could prove more difficult to achieve this, it was much less usual for schools to take specific account of home circumstances in setting homework (other than when requested perhaps by the SENCO, as indicated in Figure 2.4). The solution offered, at least in some contexts, was to provide additional support of some kind, through homework clubs or other special initiatives - a topic which will be explored more fully in 2.4.

2.4   Assessment and Feedback

We suggested in Chapter 1 that something could be learned, from schools' approach to the assessment of homework, about their commitment to making homework an integral part of their learning strategy. It is also worth noting that research evidence discussed in Appendix B suggested that homework is more likely to be associated with improvements in achievement when there is rapid and relevant feedback to pupils. But what kind of assessment and feedback for homework has proved effective in helping pupils to achieve? Does, and should, the approach vary according to the age of the pupils and the type of subject matter? And what are the implications for teachers, especially in the time they have to give to the process? So the first issue we address here is the direct impact of assessment (or lack of it) on pupils' motivation and performance. But there is a related issue: the feedback which teachers can obtain, from assessing pupils' homework, about the effect of their teaching. In other words, homework - just because it is generally completed independently of the teacher - provides invaluable evidence for evaluating the management of learning. One primary headteacher whose teachers regularly evaluated what they were doing through reviewing pupils' work made this point explicitly, in discussing differentiation: if there was a major problem, then they hadn't matched it properly, and he gave an example of how he had modified a task for the new Year 5 pupils who had clearly not understood it. We shall look first at the assessment **framework** and then at the **feedback process**.

The assessment framework

Despite the considerable differences in size, organisation and outlook, primary and secondary schools are all operating within the same national assessment framework for pupils from 5 to 16. It is therefore appropriate to ask how they fit homework and its assessment into their overall assessment framework. If, as so many schools stressed, homework is an essential component of the learning programme, how are its outcomes used to improve learning? We can start with evidence from the telephone survey.

Table 2.3 shows the responses of the primary schools. Almost all of them said they assessed homework outcomes in some way, both written work and learning tasks. Generally, written work was marked fairly quickly (half the schools said they did this by the next day), with a written comment, but less than half the schools (44%) gave a grade or mark. (The rather low percentage choosing to mention oral feedback is explained by the form of the question which was designed to elicit information mainly about more formal approaches.) Learning was always tested, usually after an interval of several days

The questions asked in secondary schools were rather different and were designed to find out if there was a single whole-school policy on assessing homework, and what it covered (Table 2.4).

Almost three-quarters of these schools said they had such a policy which included guidelines on marking homework, but less than half of those with policies (that is, 35% of all the schools) specified how soon work should be returned. Most schools without a school-level policy expected all departments to define their own. In another question, about the strategies used to encourage a positive attitude towards homework, senior managers were asked what proportion of teachers gave feedback in class. The answers were very upbeat, with at least 70% of schools reporting that all teachers did so, a response which probably reflected a general view rather than the responses of the teachers themselves.

The picture emerging from the survey, then, is that the assessment of homework was taken seriously by most schools. In the primary school sample, almost all were highly committed to prompt and

Table 2.3
Primary Schools' Approach to Assessing Homework

Assessment strategies	% of schools
Homework (written work, learning) is assessed	99
Methods of assessing written work	
Written comment	95
Identify errors and expect corrections	88
Give a mark or grade	44
Other suggestions:	
Oral feedback	14
One-to-one feedback	9
Speed of feedback for written work	
The day it is handed in	22
The next day	31
Within the same week	41
Other/not sure	6
Interval before testing learning (spelling, tables etc.)	
On the following day	19
After a longer interval	79
Other/not sure	2

N=227

*Based on answers to several questions which were answered by
all respondents
Responses in italic were unprompted; all others were responses to
prompts or questions*

*Source: Diagnostics: Telephone Survey of Primary Schools,
Oct. 1997*

Table 2.4
Secondary Schools' Approach to Assessing Homework

Policy on assessing homework assignments	% of schools
Had a school-level policy	73
Policy covered assessment methods, e.g. use of grades or written comments	69
Policy set time limits for marking and return of homework	35
No school-level policy	27
All subject departments have their own policy	19
Some subject departments have their own policy	6
All teachers spend time going over homework in class	73
All teachers give individual feedback to pupils on their homework	70

N=141

*Based on responses to four questions which were asked of all
respondents*

*Source: Diagnostics: Telephone Survey of Secondary Schools,
Oct. 1997*

appropriate feedback, but this was not always in the form of graded assessments; further analysis suggested that only about a quarter of schools treated homework unequivocally as part of formally assessed work. Secondary schools assumed that homework would be formally assessed, but differed in how assessment was managed. Again, further analysis indicated that just under a third had a fully specified whole-school policy to provide a common framework for assessing homework.

In order to find out how schools were using assessment to improve learning we looked at these issues in more detail in the schools we visited.

In **primary schools**, there were clear differences on the issue of formal assessment from schools equally committed to the value of homework as an integral part of learning.

➡ At a rural primary school which had fairly recently developed its homework policy and had worked hard to create consensus among staff and parents about the approach, the school marking policy was to try to mark with the child present, though this was getting more difficult as the volume of homework grew. Written work was always marked with written comments and guidance on improvements, and corrections required for spelling and grammar, but grades were not given. Assessment was seen as one part of the wider responsibility of responding to children's work, which was set out in the homework policy.

➡ At a large first school with a carefully structured and planned homework programme only spelling tests were formally marked. But all homework was acknowledged and valued, with written work being stuck in topic books to show it was of equal value with class work.

➡ In a suburban primary school, where there was said to be considerable status attached to homework and parental support (or pressure) was high, the class teachers tried to give individual feedback but this was not always possible. The majority of homework set was specifically assessable and would be given alphabetic grades, with an A being excellent and N 'unsatisfactory', implying the work would have to be redone.

Perhaps not surprisingly, first schools were the least likely to use grades or other formal assessments, although considerable care was often taken in reviewing pupils' work and providing feedback. Probably more important than whether grades were used is the issue of marking policy. Some primaries made it clear that written homework was assessed using the same criteria as for class work, and these were often set down in a formal marking policy. The most comprehensive approach was reported from the small rural school:

➡ Different assessment strategies were used for different types of work. Tables were assessed monthly in Years 5 and 6 and given a mark out of 50. Revision homework at the end of subject units was given a percentage and other work was marked using A-E grades, as for class work, and corrections were required. The head teacher had an interesting system for keeping a check of pupils' progress. In his markbook, test results coloured in red denoted that pupils had not done well and needed more consolidation, while those in the green zone were ready to go on to the next stage. Perhaps twice a term homework might be used to assign National Curriculum levels. Work at KS1 tended to be marked either with the pupils or the same day, while KS2 work would be given back the next day.

In a strongly contrasting environment, an inner city, multi-ethnic primary was equally insistent on clear marking in line with school policy, and in addition set English targets every half-term which were written into pupils' homework books. But the headteacher felt that more attention still needed to be given to the assessment of homework.

For most primary teachers, there was a distinction between the assessment of regular 'core' homework, which formed part of their progress in literacy and numeracy, and other topic-related work. One school showed how individual progress in multiplication tables was recorded on the basis of post-homework tests, with the results used to assign subsequent levels of work.

➡ A primary school with an established homework policy since 1993 explained the clear distinction between testing of core skills homework and the assessment of written work. No work done at home was graded, but written

work, especially in Years 5 and 6, would have careful written comments from the teacher with developmental points. Work also had to meet the school's presentation conventions - e.g. black ink had to be used and work completed in exercise books.

➡ In an outer London school, which had been very strictly managed, all work was marked and returned as soon as possible with comments on what had been achieved well and targets for further work. Assessment was done in line with the school marking policy, and pupils were also rewarded with house points for effort.

Giving feedback: meaning and manageability

Just as important as these formal systems, especially in the early years, was the dialogue on progress which **primary** teachers developed both with the child and with parents. This included oral feedback and the exchange of written comments in home-school contact books and reading records or diaries (see Figure 2.6). The effective use of these written exchanges depended on giving parents clear criteria and explanation of how comments could help their child's progress; otherwise, only a minority of parents generally went beyond the factual record that work or reading had been completed. It was notable that schools which had a strong commitment to, and a sustained investment in, partnership with parents were more likely to trust parents to provide appropriate support in later years, so that pupils' work could be validly assessed as their own effort.

Whatever the methods of assessing homework, the key issue was how effectively teachers used it to inform pupils (and their parents) and to help them to understand how to improve their performance; and also how they fed the evidence into the professional review process, to improve their own teaching. This was where clear guidelines and expectations were particularly useful, since once again they promoted consistency and provided a framework for evaluation. Other aspects of good classroom practice, such as target-setting, helped to complete the feedback loop. Teachers were asked about the time they each spent on preparing, assessing and feeding back homework to pupils. Primary schools produced figures of between one and four hours per week, with about two hours being the norm. The results suggest that they often found it difficult to separate from other work and in the majority of schools saw it as time well spent (see also Chapter 3.4).

In **secondary schools**, formal assessment of homework was the norm. Here the issue for teachers was how to make the marking of homework both meaningful and manageable, with each teacher responsible for many classes and homework usually required in most or all subjects. Visits to schools, all of which had been identified for their good practice in homework, suggest the survey findings on feedback may be optimistic. One reason for this was the amount of time which teachers reported spending on marking homework. Estimates varied from 5 to 10 hours per week, but some of these were 'guesstimates' by senior staff. Subject teachers themselves often found it difficult even to make an estimate. It was also difficult to ascertain how closely guidelines on marking were followed. In one school where the staff knew they were expected to give grades and comments on most homework, soon after it was handed in, pupils reported that this was often not the case. In another school where rapid marking and return was the policy, pupils commented that this was true in mathematics, which had a rigorous approach, but less so in other subjects. Similar discrepancies over speed and quality of feedback were noted by pupils in several other schools. Various strategies had been adopted in order to achieve the goal of making the marking of homework both meaningful and manageable. Only in a few schools had these been fully implemented.

➡ A high-achieving boys' school in London set one 'major' (usually written) and one 'minor' homework task for each subject per week and used the distinction to ease the assessment burden; only major homeworks were to be marked. The English department set out detailed guidance on marking which applied to both class work and homework, pointing out that *imaginative setting and marking of homework may reduce marking load and may free teachers to concentrate on other aspects of pupils' work*. Teachers were urged not to 'blanket mark'; instead they *should build into the plan for the task their marking strategy. They should let their pupils know what they,*

the teachers, will be marking. As an example, a teacher may wish to ignore altogether any irregularities in surface features if he or she is checking and awarding for understanding or interpretations.'

One of the survey schools had produced a booklet on 'marking and setting homework', with a number of suggested 'short cuts', including:

○ *Select one aspect: Mark in detail ONE aspect of work, e.g. opening and concluding paragraphs with the rest skimmed;*

○ *Pupils in charge: Work out a mark scheme and allow pupils to mark each others' work. Insist that they mark, comment and initial. Follow up by scrutinising 5 books in detail yourself;*

○ *Rotate detailed scrutiny: six pupils at a time, therefore everyone getting a very full commentary about once a month, with less detail at other times;*

○ *Save time finding the work: Pupils hand in books open at the appropriate page. Collect in alphabetical order.*

These and other schools wanted to make assessment meaningful, that is to ensure that it was not only linked to classroom learning but actually helped to enhance it. The art department in one school had focused clearly on this goal, with its detailed marking scheme for the planned assignments mentioned in 2.2, making the success criteria explicit not only for staff but also for pupils (see Figure 2.5).

➡ The art department's KS3 marking policy, part of a highly structured homework system, had been adopted by all the creative studies departments and was making an impact on the marking policies of other departments. The homework booklets outlined how each assignment would be assessed. Teachers worked to a common set of attainment grades, with clear criteria for marking. This also provided continuity and consistency with GCSE criteria in KS4.

In this way assessment could satisfy the principle set out by another school, that assessment should not only 'feed back' useful information to the pupil but should also 'feed forward' into subsequent learning.

Figure 2.5
Year 8 Art Homework

Extract from Record of Achievement sheet for KS3 Art

Project Title:
OBJECTIVE DRAWING/PATTERN MAKING

ATs	WHAT YOU ARE ASSESSED ON

The *Tonal Drawing* must show you can:

AT1 s1   draw with accuracy an elliptical object keeping it in proportion;

AT1 s3   use tonal shading to create form.

The *Design Sheet* must show you can:

AT1 s4   select 6 different motifs from your drawing and recognise the primary, secondary and complementary colours;

AT2 s1   choose 1 motif and create a repeat pattern from it that is accurately drawn, neatly coloured in using pencil crayon and effective as a textile design.

In talking about assessment, experienced teachers explained how they used the information gained from assessment not only to set targets for pupils but also to evaluate their own teaching. It was less usual to find managers making systematic use of such evidence to evaluate the quality of homework and its impact on the learning programme as a whole. This issue will be revisited in 3.3, in considering the strategies which schools had developed for evaluating their homework programme.

2.5 Purposeful Learning in English and Mathematics: Primary Experience

From the review so far, there have been many pointers to the ways in which homework can contribute to purposeful learning in these core areas of the curriculum. We want to draw on these ideas in order to summarise and illustrate how schools were applying their principles, which are relevant to all age groups. The evidence presented here is from primary schools, for whom these areas were the backbone of the homework programme.

Reading, writing, listening and speaking

All the schools we visited introduced homework activities related to literacy from an early stage, some even from the nursery. What varied was the degree of structure and progression in the homework programme, and the extent and type of parental collaboration that was involved. The following features of homework seemed to be associated with effective learning:

- **Sound foundations.** Schools provided workshops and materials to help parents get their children interested in reading and writing, and to practise relevant skills.

- **Regular habits.** As children embarked on reading (and being read to), schools made it clear that there should be regular home-based sessions. Some schools expected daily reading, others were happy with two or three sustained sessions a week, as long as these were seen as fixed points and provided 'quality time' for parent and child.

- **Two-way traffic.** It was common practice for teachers and parents to use a reading record or diary to record and comment on the books read. These were more purposeful when teachers indicated how the parent could help or what aspect or words to practise. This kind of dialogue flourished when teachers had involved parents from the beginning, kept them well informed about homework tasks and used opportunities to discuss their child's progress face to face (see extracts in Figure 2.6). Some schools continued the dialogue right through KS2, providing regular feedback, for example by setting and marking spelling tests in a homework book which parents saw regularly.

- **Skills for success.** Parents and children learned how to consolidate classroom learning by practising specific skills at home, in reading (for example through phonics programmes), handwriting, spelling, grammar and punctuation, with the 'rules' or targets made explicit.

- **Onward and upward.** Schools had developed clear structures for progression. These might be based on published schemes, for example for spelling, reading or grammar, or worked out by

Figure 2.6
Extracts from Reading Records

Extracts from a Reception class reading record, Autumn 1997

Date	Book	Any comments [Parent's comments in italic]
6/10	**The Apple**	He 'read' through story quite well and laughed a lot at the end when Floppy ate the apple
7/10	**Salad Days**	*He didn't have time to do it tonight - he was in bed by 5 p.m. and asleep by 5.45 p.m*
29/10	**Baa Baa Black Sheep**	A good book for discussing the difference between words and pictures.
		Jack struggled to recognise words - not helped by being extremely tired. think I was trying to do too much with him, given his lack of letter recognition. Some positive signs though e.g. 'Black' was almost like his name.
		Brilliant!
4/11	**Mary, Mary.** Please ask Jack to say the words as he matches them preferably in the right order.	All children learn to read in different styles. Jack may learn to recognise whole words before individual letters. This book is really so he can recognise the difference between a letter and a word.
7/11	**The Pet Shop**	Brilliant reading Jack!
		Read it to me - seemed to be reading well - really pleased with himself.

Extracts from Year 3 Reading Diaries, Autumn 1997

Date	Book	Any comments [Parent's comments in *italic*, child in red]
16/10	**Snow Goose**	It's getting up to an exciting part, I can tell.
29/10	**The Day Matt sold Great Grandma** (Group reading in class)	I'm encouraging Rachel to use a loud clear voice in group reading. No problems with the text.
	Snow Goose	*Read with David - fluent and enjoyable.*
		It's a bit skery.
17/10	**Clive keeps his Cool**	*For some reason large parts of this book were sung to me in an American accent..!*
28/10	**Clive keeps his Cool**	It was class.
30/10	**Grace the Pirate**	It was scarey and it was about pirates *and he thoroughly enjoyed the bit where there was a death penalty if women boarded the ship!*
		Thanks for all your help.

the school itself, but teachers of all relevant year groups understood and applied the scheme in the same way, so that progression and differentiation within and across year groups were secured.

- **Varied diet.** Although schools stressed the importance of regular learning and practice of core skills, pupils were also expected, as they got older, to use a wide range of language skills in their homework, in all four modes (reading, writing, listening and speaking), for practical tasks, imaginative projects, and all aspects of the curriculum.

- **On purpose.** Homework tasks in these schools included writing or speaking for a clear purpose and often for a real audience (including presentations to the class). Opportunities were taken to relate homework to people, events or situations outside school. In some schools, one main type of task was used to structure development in the use of language (for example, book reviews personal studies).

BOX 2.1
PROGRESS IN READING

In this pleasant junior school in a stable community, where most children came up from the infants school on the same site, there was an established and quite demanding homework programme. Year 3 were expected to spend one hour per week, with the total rising by one hour per year, to four hours per week in Year 6. These allocations included reading every night, starting off with 5 minutes in Year 3 and increasing to 15 minutes per night in Year 6. Books were differentiated according to ability and allocated on the basis of reading tests. All pupils in Years 3 and 4 took home *Reading is Fun* cards and parents signed that their child had read each night. They got stickers if they had completed the card. Years 5 and 6 had a different card and earned house points for completion. They were expected to complete three book reviews per term, based on their own choice of books.

In addition to this sustained reading programme, pupils learn spellings and by Year 6 complete one piece of written work per week, often based on the Nelson skill scheme.

BOX 2.2
SOUND FOUNDATIONS

In this rural 4 to 8 school, with 309 on roll, the main focus for homework in English and literacy was on skills. The English co-ordinator had a clear overview of what was happening through the school, there was a common pattern for homework in all classes, from Reception onwards, and all children took home books to share. To ensure that their youngest pupils could also benefit, the school had invested in a set of books for early years pupils. Parents were given guidance on helping their children with reading and there was a strong partnership between home and school. A reading meeting was held with parents of 'rising fives' to discuss pre-reading experiences and the range of strategies used by the school.

Year 1 pupils were organised into ability groups for phonics; they had a 'phonic rocket', a worksheet which also included rhyming words. They were set lists of 10 words, based on either key words or the phonics scheme to read and spell at home, using the 'phonic rocket' as a check on progress.

Year 2 pupils received spellings every week, based on word families; they also continued with the development of phonic knowledge through words sent home. The less able received sets of 5 words, the more able sets of 10. By **Year 3** the spelling lists were based on words they had used in their own work and topic-based words designed to extend their vocabulary. Spelling was given out on Friday, to learn for the following Friday. It was often tested through dictation which was felt to be a useful monitoring exercise. Particular attention was given to pupils with special needs.

Figure 2.7
Year 6 Book Review

Book Review

Introduction
The following is a review on a book which I read recently at school. The title is George's Marvellous Medicine and it was written by a famous author, renowned for writing children's stories, his name is Roald Dahl. The illustrations in the book are by Quentin Blake and I have read that he was Roald Dahl's favourite illustrator. This particular book was first published in 1981.

About the author
Roald Dahl was born in Wales in 1916 and died in 1990. The bad treatment he received as a child at school, led him to write stories about cruelty and revenge. He also wrote a number of film scripts, including Chitty Chitty Bang Bang. In total he wrote 19 childrens' books, the best known of which were James and the Giant Peach and Charlie and the Chocolate Factory.

About the book
This book is about how a young boy, called George, planned revenge for being cruelly treated by his selfish grandma. She was a sneaky person, because she acted kindly towards George when his parents were around, but when they were not, she was cruel and unkind to him.

I enjoyed reading this story, because it was so descriptive and expressive, I felt as though I was George. The way he behaved, even though it was naughty, made me feel that I would probably do the same if I were George.

Something that I did not like about the story, was how George managed to do so much in such a short time. I did not feel that his actions would have bee possible to carry out in the time, but then the story is fictional after all.

I do not think that this is Roald Dahl's best story, but I do feel that he was trying to send a clear message to the reader: to think before you act, or you might regret what you do. Revenge is never advisable, as others could get hurt and you cannot turn the clock back. I found out about this book from previous book I had read I would recommend it for younger readers.

To illustrate these principles, Boxes 2.1 and 2.2 describe the main features of language-related homework in two of the schools we visited. Primary schools were keen to stress how they worked on all aspects of language, both in the classroom and through homework, and then asked pupils to apply them to 'real' tasks such as personal studies. The goal of all this investment was that Year 6 pupils, by the time they moved on to secondary school, would not only be confident in literacy and oracy but would be able to use their skills to enhance their learning, by planning their work, weighing evidence, presenting ideas and adapting language for purpose and audience. Figure 2.7 presents a book review, written (word processed) for homework, by a Year 6 pupil in an east London school.

Numeracy and mathematical understanding

Most of the primary schools introduced homework in this area somewhat later than language-related tasks. However, some offered parents games and other simple activities which could be used from school entry, as an optional task. Many of the principles of good practice outlined above also applied here, but there was less consistency in schools' approach. Some schools relied principally on systematic learning of key elements: number bonds, tables and 'mathematics facts', gradually complementing these with practice exercises, perhaps drawn from the published scheme used in the classroom. Others, while including a strong learning component, used homework as an opportunity to carry out investigations. The most popular programme in primary schools was a published scheme of structured investigations, to be completed with some element of parental support (see Box 2.3).

There were some specific points which seemed to be associated with good practice in mathematics homework:

● **Co-ordinated programme.** The mathematics co-ordinator worked with the staff team to plan the overall structure of mathematics homework. This usually covered:

❍ when and how learning tasks would be introduced;

❍ what (published) mathematics scheme would be used (many incorporated practice and extension tasks);

❍ how work would be assessed and differentiated

Class teachers then managed the day-to-day plan within this framework

● **Realistic targets.** There was a balance between class targets (for example the number bonds or multiplication tables that should be mastered during the year) and targets for individuals. For pupils with special needs these would be set in

---

**BOX 2.3
USING A MATHEMATICS INVESTIGATION SCHEME**

The school (NOR, 210) is one of several primaries in this small town, with good levels of parental support. It received a favourable inspection report in 1997, the inspectors noting that children had good attitudes to learning on entry. The school homework policy dateD from 1993, when parents asked for more guidance on homework.

Mathematics homework started in Reception, with daily counting activities and progress in Year 1 with occasional number facts work. Number bonds, tables and 'mental mathematics' work continued through Year 2-5, with pupils sorted into three ability groups within each class, together with occasional data collection tasks for topic work. Recently a weekly mathematics assignment had been introduced for Year 6. This was based on a published scheme and was differentiated by level.

The main thrust of the mathematics homework programme, however, was the 'mathematics half term'. Years 2-5 each did 4-6 weeks of investigations, on a rota basis. This was used to support a topic focus in class (e.g. number, algebra, shape/space, data handling). Individual records were kept of work covered, with feedback and evaluation from child, parent and teacher using a pro-forma. The worksheets used a games or problem-solving approach and often required another person (parent, older sibling) to join the activity. The activities targeted specific skills and the feedback could be quite detailed (X found that if you times 2 odd numbers together, the answer is odd). Parents could also identify the exact point of difficulty, if any, helping the teacher to focus carefully. The purpose, therefore, was diagnostic and the work was not formally assessed.

The school felt the scheme could only be run for half a term each year because of the demand it made on teachers. They had to plan the work, copy sheets, insert them in wallets, mark the work, read comments and add feedback. This typically took well over an hour a week. Having the scheme on a rota also helped parents, who would only have one child doing it at once.

Interviews with children showed that Impact mathematics was very popular, at all ages. They liked the games approach to practice and reinforcement and the element of discovery. It was also popular with parents, some of whom would have liked to see it offered weekly throughout the school. Staff, too, were so convinced of its value that they had developed their own science investigations programme for KS1, on the same lines, which was currently in use with Years 2 and 3.

---

collaboration with the SENCO. Most classes were grouped by attainment for routine mathematics work, but teachers also monitored

---

**BOX 2.4
LEARNING TABLES**

Two cities, two approaches

At a primary school in west London, which had SAT results above the national average despite a wide ability range and a considerable proportion of pupils eligible for free school meals, regular homework was set in mathematics for most year groups. In order to motivate pupils, the school had set up a Tables Club. Children who had learned one set (2x, etc.) were tested on all permutations of it and then became a member of the '2x club', and got a badge. This had worked well in a school where it was sometimes hard to involve parents, some of whom did not speak English and were not literate in their own language. Moreover, many lived in very cramped conditions. Some parents had difficulty with mathematics homework and had asked for a mathematics workshop, which the school had agreed to.

At another primary school, in the north east, there was a very tightly structured approach to the teaching of number. All pupils from Year 2 upwards received table facts on Monday, copied into their homework book, and were tested on Friday. The same format was used for every year group so that they became familiar with it. This strict routine was combined with mathematics workshops - for example there was an annual workshop for all Year 3 parents (with a glass of wine!), when they were shown the methods and processes that would be taught to their children, and were given a chance to experiment. They then used the same processes at home with their children. The mathematics co-ordinator felt that structure and communication were so important that staff made an effort to ensure that the parents of any child arriving during KS2 found out about the methods they were using in mathematics.

---

individual progress and adjusted homework tasks accordingly, maintaining challenge for faster learners.

- **Consolidation and challenge.** Learning tasks were regular and consistent with clear and rapid feedback, and rewards for effort and achievement. This routine was balanced by investigations and practical tasks (see boxes 2.3 and 2.4).

- **Positive partnership.** Teachers had managed to dispel any lingering mathematics phobia among parents, and demonstrated, through workshops and other events, that it was just as manageable and enjoyable to help their children with number work as with literacy. This could include homework tasks and a wide range of ordinary home activities involving number work and mathematical concepts.

Mathematics homework was more likely than language work to be firmly based on published material or schemes. While this was valuable in providing structure and progression, it perhaps meant that only the more mathematically confident teachers were willing to venture on designing their own investigations for older pupils. Nevertheless, pupils were able to apply their numeracy in science and practical assignments, and liked the confidence in numeracy which thorough practice had brought.

2.6 Overview: Towards High Quality Homework

In this chapter we have considered the quality of homework. We have looked at the measures taken by the schools in the study, all of which had received some recent commendation for their homework practice from OFSTED, to ensure the programme would satisfy the purposes they had defined. The review has covered the range and type of homework tasks and approaches, the ways in which teachers plan homework and match it to pupils' capabilities and the types of assessment and feedback they provide for pupils. We then gave some examples of these principles in practice, in primary English and mathematics. We have also drawn attention to a number of issues which arose from the evidence. We have had in mind the underlying criterion for quality homework, that it should be designed to support and enhance learning. In this overview we want to comment briefly on three aspects of the findings before setting out brief indicators of good practice, as they emerged from the evidence.

Integrating homework into learning

Schools were clear that they wanted to make homework an integral part of the learning programme. But what did this mean in practice? Primary schools were mostly clear that it implied advance planning - on varying time-scales, by different groups. Again, most of them did not see a conflict between advance planning and classroom flexibility, because the class teacher retained the authority to decide how the plan would be applied in that classroom, and for particular children. In secondary schools the idea of pre-planning homework as a teaching team, as part of the overall learning plan, seemed relatively unfamiliar. Instead, 'integrating' homework often seemed to mean reacting on a day-by-day basis to classroom developments, with tasks devised to meet the needs of a particular class on a particular occasion. If, for example, a class of pupils (or some individuals within it), were having difficulty with a new concept, the teacher might define a homework assignment to address that problem. Some secondary schools provided specific guidance on how to integrate homework into learning, partly to discourage inappropriate 'finishing off' tasks. A few departments suggested how homework could usefully be considered at the curriculum planning stage in ways which could actually assist integration without constraining the teacher; for example, by devising in advance a bank of tasks to address problematic concepts. In other words, they implied, careful planning could make it easier for the teacher to select or adapt tasks in line with the progress made by each class. Another way of making homework integral to the learning programme was to ensure that the tasks complemented as well as supported what was done in class, rather than just expecting 'more of the same'. For the youngest pupils, mathematics games both consolidated and complemented number work in class, showing that mathematics was fun, practical and something that parents could join in with. The same principle could apply to much older pupils, with homework being used for inquiry, creative activities, extended reading and writing, as well as for the 'learning' and consolidation best done alone or with adult help. In practice it was hard for schools to ensure that homework was systematically integrated into the learning programme, even in individual classes or subjects, let alone the whole school. Discussing and agreeing what it meant and how it might be achieved was an important interim goal; there was then a firm reason for planning and for rejecting 'homework creation' practices and the unthinking resort to 'finishing off'.

Tailoring homework to individual learning

If homework was meant to complement class work, so also it was intended to meet individual learning needs. This was another principle that proved very difficult to put into practice, especially in secondary schools. There were several aspects.

The most general one related to feedback. Pupils and parents wanted to know if the response offered was on the right lines: what was good, what was poor and what was lacking. Teachers were aware how challenging it was to respond to pupils individually. But good advice was available on this, and clearly the method changed according to age. Indeed, helpful and timely comments on work in progress (for longer assignments) might be more valued by pupils than grades or judgements on the finished product, particularly if these took time to appear. Most primary teachers expected to differentiate the skills development element of homework, by selecting appropriate levels of work from a multi-level scheme - usually for groups rather than for individuals. This was much less usual in secondary classes, although different tasks might well be devised for different sets; teachers were more likely to talk about 'differentiation by outcome', setting the same task for all and expecting a range of performance. Finally, there was the challenging issue of progression. Again, this was relatively easy to manage within a literacy or numeracy homework programme which embraced all age groups; individuals could 'move up' the scheme at a suitable pace. Otherwise it was hard to ensure that pupils were learning to take on harder challenges, rather than just repeating the same kind of task with slightly different content.

Building a learning partnership?

In general, primary schools were convinced that a successful homework programme depended on a strong partnership with parents; at the same time, such a partnership offered the school opportunities for putting over their ideas on learning to parents. Successful schools made it clear that in practice it was a three-way partnership, bringing in the pupil from an early age. By the secondary stage, the balance had shifted, with the pupil-teacher partnership being central, and parents being assigned a mainly supportive role. There were many unresolved questions and potential conflicts here. While many parents responded enthusiastically to the invitation to work with teachers in helping their children to learn, through homework, what were schools to do about the parents unwilling or apparently unable to take part? Was the school to act as a surrogate parent, or make more effort to include all parents? When and how did parental 'help' become inappropriate? What were parents to do when they were unable to help or support, because the task had been poorly defined?

Equally important was the challenge of teaching pupils, over time, the skills needed for effective independent learning. Undoubtedly, families could help here, especially if teachers showed them what they could do to help their children develop these skills. The idea of a common task, such as a book review or project, undertaken in each KS2 class with increasing challenges in structure and management, is a powerful one; it offers progression for the pupil and shows parents the changing nature of the help they are expected and indeed encouraged to offer. It is equally important - however difficult to manage - that the skills which pupils have developed by the end of primary school are recognised and extended in KS3.

Teachers were intensely concerned about the quality of homework, insisting that this was what mattered if homework was to contribute to learning. But as we shall see in the next chapter, much of the management effort in practice seemed to go on organising the programme and seeing requirements were met, rather than on evaluating quality. Perhaps, as some teachers suggested, the important discussion on quality went on more informally, within staff teams. However it is done, it has to be planned for, if quality issues are to stay at the top of the agenda.

INDICATORS OF GOOD PRACTICE

Primary Schools

Integrating homework and class work

- Staff teams plan homework together and alongside their schemes of work.

- There is a common whole-school framework and possibly common materials to support progression for all pupils in the core skills of literacy and numeracy; all teachers and pupils are familiar with the 'rules'.

- Other relevant staff teams (e.g. year, subject) plan topic/subject-related homework, relating it to schemes of work.

- The SENCO is fully involved in homework planning and provides expert comment on its feasibility (not just for pupils with SEN).

Tailoring homework to individual learning

- Core skills tasks are differentiated to maximise progression for all pupils.

- All pupils have the chance to undertake a wide range of tasks (including enrichment activities).

- Tasks are designed to make an equal demand on all pupils; this means that the difficulty may vary, but the time and effort required are broadly the same.

- For pupils with SEN, the balance of skills development and other work is planned together by SENCO and class teacher, and discussed with parents.

- Assessment and feedback is prompt and works to agreed whole-school criteria.

Building a partnership with parents

- Teachers collaborate closely with parents on home-based learning, explaining aims and methods and showing them how to help their children.

- Parents are kept fully informed about homework plans.

- The school encourages parents to play a full part by providing relevant workshops and other forms of support.

Developing independent learners

- Pupils learn to manage and structure their homework tasks, moving gradually from simple activities to more complex, open-ended assignments.

- Pupils learn to manage homework time, by working to varying deadlines.

- Pupils become competent in using a range of resources (e.g. people, print, objects, IT), from school and home.

Secondary Schools

Integrating homework and class work

- Staff subject teams plan homework resources alongside their schemes of work.

- The range of homework tasks is both varied and balanced.

- Homework complements class work, e.g. by focusing on other relevant tasks which require more time or reflection, or in consolidating skills; it is very seldom for 'finishing off' class work.

- The SENCO is fully involved in departmental homework planning and provides expert comment on its feasibility (not just for pupils with SEN).

Tailoring homework to individual learning

- All pupils have the chance to undertake a wide range of tasks (including enrichment activities).

- Tasks are designed to make an equal demand on all pupils in the class; this may well mean varying the skills level or approach for groups or individuals, but the time and effort required are broadly the same for all.

- Assessment and grading are based on agreed whole-school and departmental criteria.

- Pupils are aware of these criteria, and are told the specific assessment criteria for subject homework assignments.

- Feedback is prompt, includes comments, and advice/requirements (e.g. corrections, targets) are specific.

- For pupils with SEN, the balance of skills development and other work is planned together by SENCO and subject teacher, and shared with parents.

Building a partnership with parents

- Teachers explain to parents how they can help their children.

- Parents are kept fully informed about homework plans and pupils' progress.

- Tasks are clearly explained, so pupil and parent can both understand them.

Developing independent learners

- There is a KS3/KS4 programme to develop independent learning skills.

- Pupils learn to manage homework time, by working to varying deadlines.

- Pupils become competent in using a range of resources (e.g. people, print, objects, IT), from school and home, independently.

- There is some attempt to co-ordinate the skills required for homework, across subjects.

3 Managing the Homework Programme

In this chapter the focus moves from the quality of homework, as an element of the learning programme, to the more procedural aspects, including the quantity of work which is set (3.1) and the rules, procedures and resources for organising the homework programme (3.2). It also reviews how managers develop and sustain a strategy for homework, including defining a policy, sharing it with teachers, pupils and parents, and evaluating its effectiveness (3.3). The last topic considered is the investment which schools make to support their regular homework programme and - in some cases - to contribute to other initiatives to develop out-of-class learning (3.4). Lessons learned from all these aspects are then reviewed (3.5)

Schools invest considerable effort in their procedures for structuring homework allocations and ensuring that the work is set and completed, with (in some cases) quite complex rewards and sanctions. Within school documents, these procedures are often described in more detail than the systems for planning and evaluating the quality of homework, perhaps partly because they involve a wider range of participants - pupils, parents and governors as well as teachers. Equally, it is easier to measure and analyse the time allocated to homework, for different age groups or schools, than to evaluate its quality. These are important matters, but only insofar as they affect the outcomes of homework - its impact on learning. It is hoped that the criteria defined in earlier chapters will provide a framework for reviewing the relevance and appropriateness of the allocations and procedures considered here.

3.1   How Much Homework?

Appendix B shows that considerable research effort has been expended on measuring homework time (time allocated and time spent) and attempting to correlate this with performance outcomes. It also shows that it is difficult to obtain reliable measures, or indeed to know how schools (or countries) decide what is an appropriate amount. We know that in England in particular there have been wide variations between schools in the amount of homework set, but also that the allocation increases as pupils get older. Through this study we could address the question: how much homework is allocated by schools which have been commended for their homework (or overall) practice? And what do pupils in some of these schools have to say about the time they spend on homework?

Time allocations

The basic currency for organising homework relates to quantity, expressed as time and/or frequency (minutes per subject, minutes or hours per night or per week, numbers of occasions per week). In their policies, schools usually set down the amount of homework that was expected, though with varying degrees of precision. Many primary schools, in our experience, were reluctant to specify precise time allocations, preferring to indicate which tasks were to be performed, and how often each would be set. This might be accompanied by a time guideline such as 'not more than 20 minutes'.

Just under half (45%) of the primary schools responding to the telephone survey said they did not have a homework timetable with times and tasks tied down to specific days. In secondary schools, a homework timetable was the norm, setting down the subjects to be studied each night and either a general rubric on time (e.g. 30 minutes per subject) or a specified time allocation for every homework 'slot'. But the guidelines often indicated that a measure of flexibility was to be expected, both in the actual amount of time pupils might spend and the timing and scope of particular assignments. However precise the specification might appear, therefore, it seemed to be generally expected that time allocations would always be estimates rather than exact requirements. Teachers' allocations nevertheless remain a useful currency because they indicate what school planners and subject specialists think is appropriate, if homework is to fulfil its purpose in enhancing learning.

Appendix B looks at the international evidence on these issues, and shows how difficult it is to make valid comparisons. Nevertheless, some patterns emerge, in comparing practice in England with that in other countries. In particular, English primary pupils were apparently given less homework than those in many other countries. At secondary level, there was less difference, and in science it seemed that English pupils were actually expected to do more homework. The most striking finding was the wide international range of results for specific subjects, as indicated in the Third International Mathematics and Science Study (TIMSS).

Weekly totals. Here we want to start by focusing on the total weekly time allocated for homework for each year group in order to summarise the differences within schools, for different age groups, and between schools. The data comes mainly from the telephone survey, in which head teachers were asked for some detailed information on time allocations.

Figure 3.1 shows, for each of four year groups, the time (in minutes) allocated per week by a range of schools - those lying between the 25th and the 75th percentile of the overall distribution. This form of presentation indicates the spread among

the 'middle' group of schools and shows where the 'average' (median) school comes within this range. It is clear that among this middle group, of a sample which had all been commended for their practice, the range was considerable, especially in the secondary schools. In Year 3, it was between one and two hours, but by Year 10 the weekly total for this 'middle' group of schools was between 8 hours 45 minutes and 11 hours 15 minutes, or (in daily terms) between 1 hour 45 minutes and 2 hours 15 minutes a day. These differences, if strictly observed, would result in an extra one hundred home study hours a year.

The differences over all the schools in the survey (rather than just the 'middle' group) are shown in Table 3.1, which groups the total time per week for the four year groups.

Figure 3.1
Weekly Homework Allocations (in minutes) for Four Year Groups: Inter-quartile Range

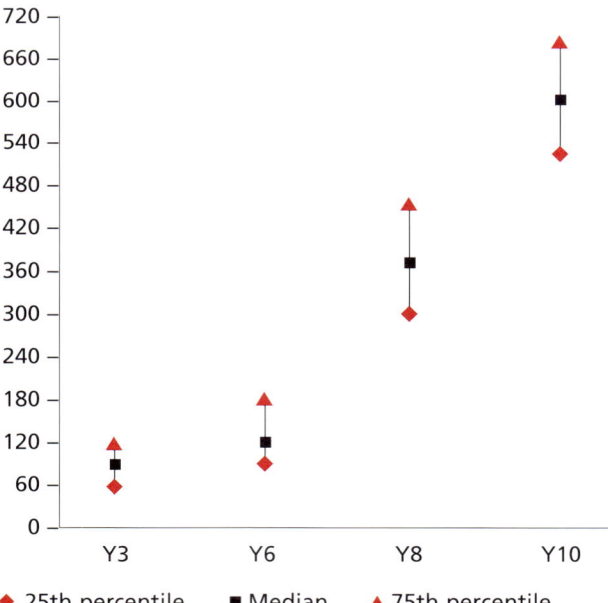

◆ 25th percentile   ■ Median   ▲ 75th percentile

All schools with the relevant year groups and providing data: Y3 (208), Y6(185), Y8(131) Y10 (138)

Source: Diagnostics Telephone Survey of 227 Primary and 141 Secondary Schools, Oct. 1997

Table 3.1
Weekly Homework Allocation for Four Year Groups

Hours per week	Y3 % of schools	Y6 % of schools	Y8 % of schools	Y10 % of schools
< 1 hour	14	5		
1 <1.5 hours	26	11		
1.5 <2 hours	26	18	1	
2 <3 hours	27	34	4	
3 <4 hours	6	20	5	1
4 <5 hours		12	2	0
5 <6 hours			24	5
6 <7 hours			18	2
7 <8 hours			33	12
8 <9 hours			6	10
9 <10 hours			1	4
10 <11 hours			5	30
11 <12 hours			1	11
12+ hours				25
N	208	185	131	138

Based on all those schools with the relevant year groups responding to the question
Percentages may not all sum to 100 because of rounding

Source: Diagnostics Telephone Survey of Primary and Secondary Schools, Oct. 1997

The results again show that, in each phase, there was more consensus about the allocation for the younger of the two age groups. In Year 10 the lack of consensus shows up clearly. Does this reflect the ability level of the pupils or simply different approaches to planning homework for KS4? Further analysis of the time allocation data suggested that there was no clear trend linking time allocated to homework in each phase with performance levels in national tests or GCSE. Schools with higher average performance in KS2 tests were likely to set more homework, but the association was not statistically significant.

The other finding clearly demonstrated in Figure 3.1 and Table 3.1 is the increase in time allocations with pupil age. The median weekly totals - the amount allocated by the school or schools at the halfway point in the distribution - indicate this increase, particularly from primary to secondary. Another way of showing the increase is presented in Figure 3.2 which plots the mean weekly total allocated for each year group, as reported by primary and secondary schools.

Figure 3.2
Weekly Homework Time Allocations: Means for each Year Group

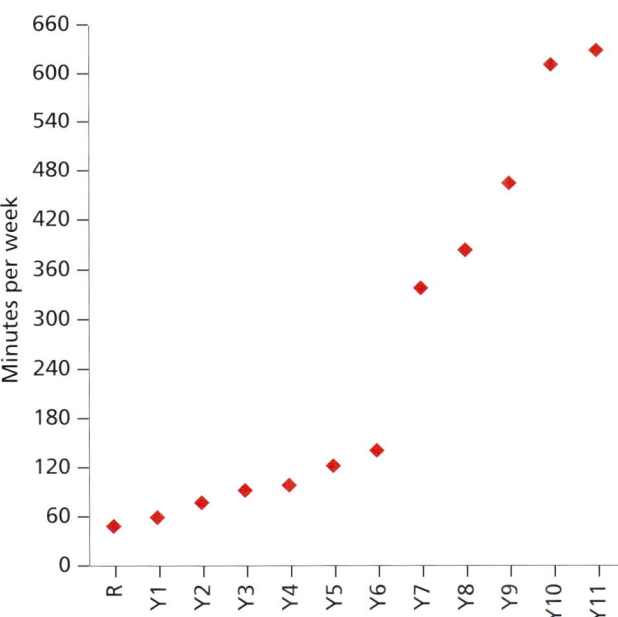

Source: Diagnostics Telephone Survey of Primary and Secondary Schools, Oct. 1997

The graph shows a steady but gradual increase over the primary years, up to an average of just under 2½ hours in Year 6. There is then a massive jump to a mean weekly total of 6½ hours a week

in Year 7, and annual increases become steadily larger up to Year 10. The gradient from the end of KS3 (Year 9) to the beginning of KS4 is particularly steep, with an average increase of 1½ hours a week.

Case study evidence on time allocations shows how difficult it can be, on the ground, to obtain valid figures. There were some difficulties in computing weekly allocations at the secondary schools we visited, but it appeared these were within the range of the 'middle group' of survey schools for KS3. The situation was much less clear for most primaries. Some almost took for granted the daily 15 minutes or so which they expected pupils to spend on reading, listing time allocations only for 'formal' homeworks, for example three tasks of 20 minutes each per week in Years 3 to 5 and three of 30 minutes in Year 6. Two schools had set down total weekly figures for each year group, as shown below:

Year group	School 1 Minutes per week	School 2 Minutes per week
Reception	60	50
Year 1	90	50
Year 2	180	120
Year 3	180	140
Year 4	180	140
Year 5	180	160
Year 6	240	200

However, these schools were in the minority, not only in specifying time in this way but also in the quantity of regular homework set. Other schools had a lighter timetable of regular tasks, combined with extended assignments for KS2 pupils which could certainly take up a great deal of time.

Subject allocations. The other aspect of homework allocation relates to the time specified for each subject per week. In the telephone survey, this was only asked of secondary schools (primary schools were asked how regularly homework was set in each subject area). Figure 3.3 overleaf shows the weekly average for subject areas, for Year 8 and Year 10 pupils.

Figure 3.3
Average Weekly Subject Allocations in Secondary Schools

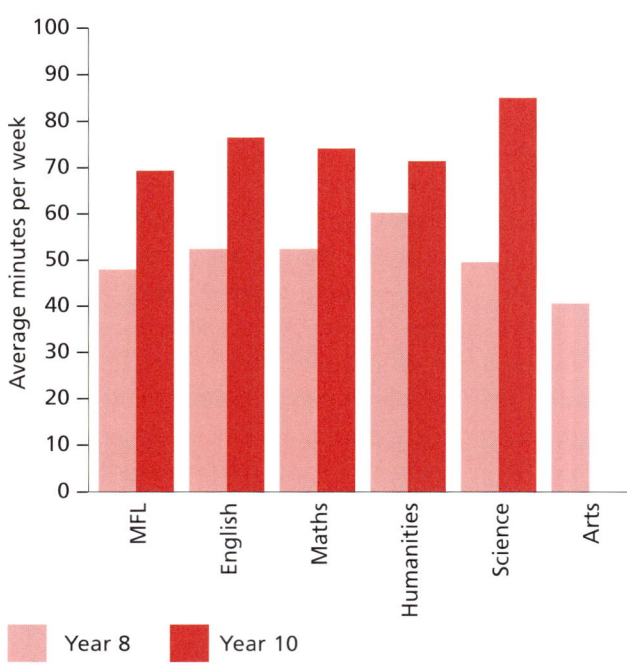

Year 8   Year 10

Source: Diagnostics Telephone Survey of 141 Secondary Schools, Oct. 1997

The graph suggests that, for each year group, average allocations were fairly similar for each subject: about 45-60 minutes for Year 8 and just over an hour for Year 10. Only Y8 science (85 minutes) and English (77 minutes) had more. However, the detailed results (Table 3.2) suggest these averages masked considerable variations, both within and between subjects. In Year 8, humanities were the subject areas where there was least agreement about what counted as an appropriate allocation, with half the schools specifying an hour or less, and the other half over an hour. In over a third of schools very little time was allocated to homework in the arts - less than half an hour per week. By Year 10, there was a more consistent pattern for the five areas shown, although nearly half the schools (45%) set over 90 minutes of science homework, perhaps because it was seen as a 'double' subject. More striking is the variation in totals for most subjects, with substantial minorities of schools apparently satisfied with less than an hour per week while others expected over 90 minutes.

Table 3.2
Subject Allocations for Homework

Year 8

Minutes	MFL % of schools	English % of schools	Mathematics % of schools	Humanities % of schools	Science % of schools	Arts % of schools
<30	18	4	5	16	10	35
31-60	54	67	67	33	60	43
61-90	16	19	18	33	20	9
90+	6	4	4	12	4	4
No response	6	6	6	7	7	9

N=141

Year 10

Minutes	MFL % of schools	English % of schools	Mathematics % of schools	Humanities % of schools	Science % of schools
<30	3	0	0	1	0
31-60	33	25	28	38	16
61-90	40	41	41	32	35
90+	21	32	29	26	45
No response	3	2	2	4	2

N=141

Source: Diagnostics Telephone Survey of 141 Secondary Schools, Oct. 1997

Table 3.3 Frequency of Homework within Subject Areas, Years 3 and 6

Frequency	English		Mathematics		Humanities		Science		Arts	
	Y6	Y3	Y6	Y3	Y6	Y3	Y6	Y3	Y6	Y3
	% of schools		% of schools		% of schools		% of schools		% of schools	
Regularly	92	90	81	71	17	8	22	9	3	2
Often	7	7	12	16	27	15	23	13	7	7
Occasionally	1	2	6	12	55	68	52	69	72	69
Never	0	0	0	0	0	6	3	9	17	25
No response	1	1	1	1	1	2	1	0	2	2
N=	199	225	199	225	199	225	199	225	199	225

All those with the relevant year group and setting homework
Due to rounding, percentages may not always sum to 100

Source: Diagnostics Telephone Survey of Primary Schools, Oct. 1997

While primary schools were asked mainly about the frequency with which homework was set within subject areas, rather than time allocations, their responses (Table 3.3) showed clearly that, even in KS2, English and mathematics were the only subjects for which homework was regularly set (by 70% or more of schools).

In Year 3, less than 20% set homework in the other subject areas (humanities, science, arts) more than 'occasionally'. Head teachers were asked to estimate the weekly time allocations for English and mathematics for these years, but in each case some were unable to do so. For the rest, estimated time allocations were higher for English than mathematics in each year group (Table 3.4).

The variation between schools was even more marked than in secondary schools. If these estimates are even approximately right, they suggest that Year 6 pupils in many of these schools were expected to spend at least as much homework time on these two subjects as would be expected in Year 7.

Further light was shed on subject allocations during our visits to schools. Almost all the secondary schools we visited had a homework timetable but allocations could not always be straightforwardly computed from the timetable. There were several parameters to consider: how long should a pupil work each evening? How long should be spent on one subject assignment? How many assignments should there be for each subject per week? Some schools took the line that there should be one assignment per subject per week,

Table 3.4
Weekly Homework Allocations for English and Mathematics: Years 3 & 6

Minutes	English		Mathematics	
	Year 3	Year 6	Year 3	Year 6
	% of schools		% of schools	
< 30	5	3	23	10
30-59	31	32	34	40
60-89	27	24	14	22
90-119	11	13	6	8
120 or more	7	15	2	5
Don't know	18	14	22	15
Average (in minutes)	64	73	44	55
N=	223	198	222	198

All those with the relevant year group and setting homework
Due to rounding, percentages may not always sum to 100

Source: Diagnostics Telephone Survey of Primary Schools, Oct. 1997

giving 10 or 11 assignments. In one technology college this approach applied to the whole of KS3, with the time for each assignment increasing from 20 minutes in Year 7 to 30 in Year 8 and 45 in Year 9. In others, more homework time was given to core subjects. A new head of foreign languages in one school decided to split the single assignment into two shorter ones, in order to separate off some time for learning tasks. The most structured approach was found in the London school which required weekly major assignments (one for most NC subjects) and minor homeworks (one for each academic subject). However, staff in some schools were not always aware of the time allocations for each year group. Moreover, staff and pupils often recognised that the homework timetable was more of a guideline than a precise requirement, with longer assignments being set in some subjects than was indicated on the homework timetable. One school set out its expectations for each subject at some length in guidelines for parents, but with little guidance on time. For English, for example, the Year 7 guidelines stated that *'One written homework will be set each week and students will be given work to do after each lesson. They should also read for at least twenty minutes each day'*. However, the school policy suggested that each assignment should take about 30 minutes. There was certainly a marked contrast between the rather flexible approach to the timetabling of homework in this school and the tightly monitored system at some other schools. Flexibility put the onus on pupils to manage their tasks; clear and enforced rules obliged both staff and pupils to comply

Total time spent on homework: pupil reports

In Appendix B we note that the other way of quantifying homework volume is to find out how much time is actually spent on it. In practice, this means asking pupils, with the inevitable result that there will be considerable variations among pupils even within the same school, year group and class. Nevertheless, average figures give a point of comparison with teacher allocations. In this study, pupils in case study schools were asked in a questionnaire about the frequency of homework and the time spent on it. The results confirmed the trend for homework allocations to increase with age, but there were other findings as well.

Secondary schools certainly expected a daily homework routine, but the pupil responses suggested that this was not always fulfilled. Of the KS3 pupils, almost half (42%) said they did homework 'several days a week' rather than 'every day' (58%). In KS2 there was more variation, reflecting differences in school policies. Only one fifth of the pupils (21%) reported a daily assignment, with another 43% doing homework several days a week.

Table 3.5
Frequency of Homework, by Year Group

Frequency of homework in this class	Year 5 % of pupils	Year 6 % of pupils	Year 7 % of pupils	Year 8 % of pupils
Every day	10	23	50	67
Several days each week	44	48	50	34
At least once a week	43	28	0	0
Now and then - not every week	4	2	0	0
No response	0	0	0	0
N=	103	426	195	191

p= <.001
Due to rounding errors, percentages do not always sum to 100

Source: OFSTED KS2/KS3 Pupil Survey, Autumn 1997

Table 3.5 shows the reported frequency of homework for pupils in each year group surveyed, and the increase by age shows up clearly. Only 10% of Year 5 reported daily homework, but by Year 8 the figure had risen to two-thirds (it is surprising that it was not higher). It must be remembered, moreover, that the schools attended by these pupils all had a strong commitment to homework.

An indication of how wide the variations might be in a random sample of schools is given by responses to a question about Year 6 homework. For current Year 6 pupils, the figures were as shown in the last table. But for KS3 pupils, who were asked about homework in their last year at primary school, the figures look very different (Table 3.6). Even allowing for some bias and poor recall, the results suggest that, across the range of primary schools attended by these pupils, homework allocations were very diverse indeed, with many setting little or no regular homework. Less than a fifth of Year 7 pupils and only just over a quarter of Year 8 apparently recalled having homework more than once a week in Year 6, and between a quarter and a fifth said they had had no homework.

Pupils were also asked how much time they had spent on homework in the previous week, with the aim of getting a reasonably accurate estimate (Table 3.7).

Table 3.6
Frequency of Homework in Year 6: Comparison of Responses by KS2 and KS3 pupils

Frequency of homework in	Current Year 6 % of pupils	Current Year 7 % of pupils	Current Year 8 % of pupils
Every day	23	4	3
Several days each week	48	8	14
At least once a week	28	32	20
Now and then - not every week	2	32	41
I had no homework	0	24	21
N=	426	195	191

p= <.001
Due to rounding errors, percentages do not always sum to 100

Source: OFSTED KS2/KS3 Pupil Survey, Autumn 1997

The figures suggest that either pupils found it hard to recall a whole week's homework time, or that there was a very considerable disparity between time they considered they spent on homework and the schools' stated time allocation. For example, two thirds of primary schools in the telephone survey expected Year 6 pupils to do two hours or more per week, while only a quarter of pupils in these equally demanding schools reported doing this much. In Years 7 and 8 almost all schools expected pupils to complete at least four hours homework in the week, but only 31% of Year 7 and 45% of Year 8 pupils recalled doing over three

hours. It is unfortunately impossible to tell whether such discrepancies were the result of less homework being set than was specified in the homework timetable, or less time being spent (or recalled) by pupils than their teachers intended. The TIMSS survey of Year 9 pupils in England asked about time spent on homework *per day* for all subjects and this certainly produced higher figures with 70% doing at least an hour a day, or at least five hours per week. However, our survey certainly showed the predictable increase with age and more particularly with the move to secondary school. Of course, factors other than age and school expectations may affect the time which pupils spend. In our survey, there was a slight tendency for girls to spend more time than boys and a much clearer positive link between time spent and level of home background (measured by the number of books in the home).

Schools are well aware that pupils differ considerably in the amount of time they take to complete homework tasks, and indeed their commitment to do the work thoroughly and on time. We therefore asked senior managers in the telephone survey to estimate what proportion of their pupils tended to 'over-perform', spending longer or doing more than expected (Figure 3.4). Over a third of primary schools (38%) and over half the secondary schools (54%) estimated that at least half their pupils spent longer or did more than expected. If this is the case, then time allocations were in practice greater in those

Table 3.7
Pupils' Reports of Time spent on Homework 'Last Week'

Time on homework last week	Year 3/4 % of pupils	Year 5 % of pupils	Year 6 % of pupils	Year 7 % of pupils	Year 8 % of pupils
Less than 30 minutes	29	11	9	na	na
30 - 60 minutes	27	43	28	17	10
1-2 hours	19	25	37	24	13
Over 2 hours	22	21	25	na	na
2 - 3 hours	na	na	na	28	33
Over 3 hours	na	na	na	31	45
No response	4	0	1	1	1
N=	86	103	426	195	191

p= <.001
Due to rounding errors, percentages do not always sum to 100
na= not asked

Source: OFSTED KS2/KS3 Pupil Survey, Autumn 1997

schools than the official version suggested. Further analysis suggested that in secondary schools this 'pupil commitment' factor might be positively associated with performance levels in KS3 tests and GCSE. One interpretation could be that some high-performing schools expected pupils to meet - or even exceed - homework targets, even if this meant they spent more than the specified time on it. While it must be stressed that these results were based on staff estimates, not direct measures, of pupil time, this finding certainly raises questions about staff and pupil expectations. In Chapter 4 we shall look at the impact of homework on pupils, where the perceived demand increased significantly as pupils moved up the school.

Figure 3.4
Proportion of Pupils Thought by Schools to be 'Over-performing' in Homework

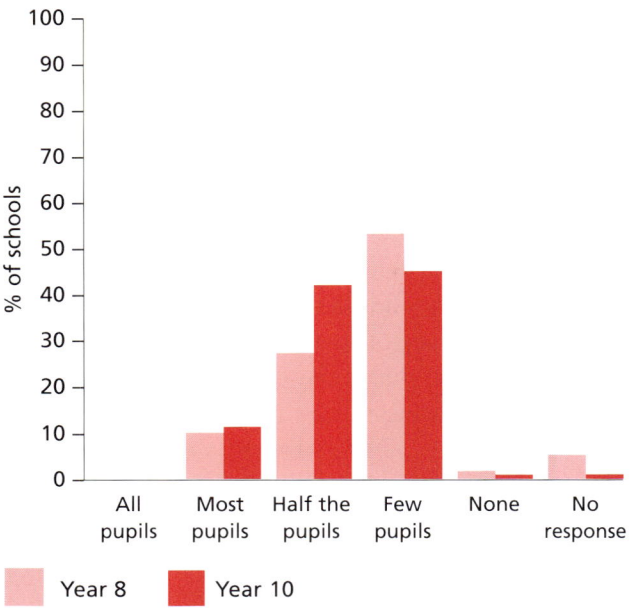

Source: Diagnostics Telephone Survey of Primary and Secondary Schools, Oct. 1997

Thinking about time

The evidence about the quantity of homework, from both survey and interview data, suggests that some hard questions need to be asked about the way homework volume is defined, an issue which is closely related to conclusions about its purpose. It is perhaps worth summarising the main parameters here.

Total time per day. Defining homework allocation in this way suggests that it is intrinsically beneficial for the pupil to spend a reasonable period in study outside the classroom, on useful tasks. It is generally expected that this period will get longer as the child gets older. Sometimes the period is seen more flexibly as a weekly allocation, to be fitted in around other commitments.

Task-led. This is a common approach to defining homework allocations in primary schools. The basic units consist of specified tasks which nearly always start with reading (often daily), usually expand to include spelling, number facts and tables, and may include phonic work, handwriting and other skills. Sometimes time allocations are suggested for tasks, but usually only for parents' guidance. Sometimes longer regular tasks such as book reviews or personal studies are added within the same framework. What matters is the task definition and deadline, rather than a precise time allocation.

Subject-led. The basic unit in most secondary schools is the subject assignment, which can be seen as an allocation of some additional learning time to be used as each subject team thinks fit. What matters to the subject teacher, therefore, is how many units or slots per week each subject receives and then what it is used for. The precise time allocated to the unit is seen as less important. The key difference from the primary school approach is that there is usually no one person to co-ordinate all these assignments, in order to assess the range of skills and tasks demanded, or indeed whether the total is reasonable. While it seems generally accepted that each subject has a claim to homework time, in practice allocations for arts and technology are variable.

In reaching decisions about how much homework should be set, schools have to weigh up the usefulness of these different measures of 'volume', in the knowledge that this can never be more than an approximate guide to the actual time pupils spend on out-of-class study. Measuring allocations in minutes was seen to have its value for staff, parents and pupils, particularly in indicating the time to be spent on tasks with no natural time limit, such as reading or learning spellings, tables or vocabulary. It was particularly important, some schools suggested, to set a time limit for pupils with SEN, who often worked more slowly and could easily be overburdened. It also set a clear framework and limits with which subject departments were expected to comply. But the neat homework timetables, which were designed to ensure that KS3 pupils had an overall limit on their nightly allocation, could only work either with very strict 'policing' (of pupils and teacher compliance) or by teaching pupils from the outset how to manage their time by spreading their work over the week. More often, the system was subject to considerable fluctuations, with some subjects not setting work on every occasion it was timetabled, while others, particularly in the humanities, sometimes set complex assignments which took far more time than had been allocated. Most pupils seemed to learn how to manage these irregularities, and one school set out clear procedures for pupils wanting to complain about over-long assignments..

Most primary schools approached time allocations rather differently. Except at certain times - for example when a deadline was approaching for a topic assignment, or pupils were 'revising for SATs' - it was unlikely that most pupils would be spending excessive time on homework. What was more important, most schools felt, was to establish the habit of regular work. To ensure this, some schools were very firm in their scheduling of regular tasks, particularly for those tested weekly (spelling and number facts). Some chose to set reading on certain days (e.g. Monday, Wednesday and Friday) after the first few years, arguing that this was more likely to be effective for children and parents than the 'daily dose'. Longer or more open-ended assignments were generally measured by 'elapsed time', with a deadline set a week or several weeks ahead, rather than by a suggested time allocation. (Interestingly, this approach seems nearer to that used in secondary schools with much older pupils, for GCSE work in KS4). However, there were primary schools which very consciously set timed subject assignments in Year 6, partly in order to prepare pupils for the demands of the secondary school homework timetable.

There are indications, however, that time allocations were important more as a management tool for ensuring fair play and informing parents

than as a precise schedule. For example, there seemed to be remarkably little debate in schools about time allocations for each secondary year group, as long as these were within well-accepted limits and followed the convention that allocations should increase with age, which was also seldom challenged. Many of the primary schools we visited, all with active homework programmes, felt strongly that defining homework by time allocation, particularly in terms of minutes to be spent each day, would actually be counter-productive. National and international surveys suggest that there is little agreement about appropriate daily or weekly allocations, overall or for particular age groups.

There are reasons for suggesting that, while there would be value in more active debate about time allocations and their 'fit' with the time actually spent by pupils, for educational purposes it may be more productive to focus on other measures of quantity, related to the type of tasks set for homework and the requirements of each subject. This would involve discussion of the balance of tasks and skills set within and across subject areas, their frequency, regularity and volume and, secondarily, the time limits which are appropriate. This would be easier to manage in primary schools, where the class teacher usually manages and monitors the whole curriculum, and where homework is more often task-led. However, in that setting, too, it is important to be clear about how, and by whom, decisions on allocations are made. In all schools it would involve senior managers and subject leaders in a review of how quantity is related to quality in their homework programme.

3.2 Managing the System

Whatever decisions schools had reached on homework allocations, almost all of them had drawn up procedures and protocols, formal or informal, for managing the homework process. These usually covered the logistics - when and how work should be set, when and how written work should be completed and handed in and the associated rewards and sanctions - and some dealt with other aspects such as marking and feedback. There was also a whole series of tools to facilitate homework management, including diaries or planners for pupils and guidance for pupils and their parents. But there were other issues to be resolved if the homework system was to work smoothly, not least the question of **control and responsibility,** with which we shall start.

Control and responsibilities

There are decisions to be made about homework at many levels. The striking feature of schools with well-established homework programmes was the consistency of the system: pupils, teachers and parents all gave the same account of how the programme worked. It was true that in these schools there was usually evidence of strong leadership from the head, but the system still depended on consensus which in some cases had taken time to achieve. In practice, an effective way of sustaining this consensus was to give a senior member of staff - often the deputy head - responsibility for co-ordinating and monitoring the homework programme.

In secondary schools most staff had a dual responsibility for homework: planning and managing work in their own subject for the classes they taught and monitoring the overall homework programme of the pupils in their tutor group or form. In the schools we visited, the tutor's role varied; there was generally an expectation that the tutor would check that homework had been completed, and any planners or notebooks kept up to date, but only in a few cases were clear criteria set out in the homework policy.

At a boys' comprehensive, tutors were expected to monitor the homework diaries weekly,

1. *To see that homework is being set and recorded;*

2. *To check that the diary is being signed by the parent;*

3. *To note and respond to any comments written in diaries by parents.*

It was acknowledged that tutors varied in the thoroughness with which they checked these diaries but the system seemed an effective one when fully implemented.

This school had provided these and indeed specified with some care the differing responsibilities of staff members (Box 3.1).

BOX 3.1
STAFF RESPONSIBILITIES FOR MANAGING HOMEWORK IN A BOYS' COMPREHENSIVE SCHOOL

The homework policy had sections setting out the responsibilities of pupils, teachers and parents. What follows is a summary of the teachers' section.

a. Tutors

- to introduce homework to pupils as part of the PSE programme
- to check homework journals [see above]
- to report problems to Head of Year (e.g. non-completion or homework not set)

b. Heads of Year

- to design homework timetable for year group
- to inform parents about homework
- to handle non-compliance (by pupils)
- to discuss teacher non-compliance with head of department
- to monitor tutors, see they are checking journals

c. Subject teachers

- to set homework according to the timetable
- to ensure homework forms a coherent part of class work
- to explain task fully, with written guidelines if possible
- to provide a summary for journals with a submission date (not next day)
- to record every homework set (and pupil non-compliance)
- to mark and return all homework promptly
- to inform head of department, tutor and head of year about persistent non-compliance

d. Heads of department

- to ensure homework is set, recorded and marked regularly
- to devise a departmental policy, in line with school policy
- to monitor teachers' records, pupils' journals and books half-termly
- to liaise with subject teachers, tutors and heads of year on pupil non-compliance
- to consult with curriculum area managers about teacher non-compliance

e. Curriculum area managers

- to ensure heads of department are monitoring the setting, recording and marking of homework each half term

f. Deputy heads

- to ensure the heads of year are monitoring pupils' effective use of journals

It was unusual for tutors to have any role in evaluating the quality of the task which had been set. This was generally seen to be the preserve of the subject department; in practice this often meant that responsibility was largely devolved to classroom teachers. We saw in Chapter 2 that, in both primary and secondary schools, class teachers often had considerable responsibility for almost all aspects of homework management, from planning to setting, marking and evaluating. There was more opportunity for monitoring the quality of the programme when this responsibility was shared with all those with an interest, including subject leaders and SENCOs.

Responsibility was further shared with **pupils and parents**, in this case mainly for ensuring that homework was satisfactorily completed and (where appropriate) returned. In the telephone survey of secondary schools, senior managers were asked about the role of various groups in ensuring that homework was completed. Table 3.8 shows the results.

Table 3.8
Secondary Schools: Responsibility for Ensuring Homework is Completed

	Major role % of school	Some responsibility % of schools	No role/no information % of schools
Pupils	97	3	0
Subject teachers	99	0	1
Parents	48	50	2
Tutors	39	60	1
Mentors	14	40	46
N=141			

140 respondents answered at least one of these questions
Due to rounding, percentages may not always sum to 100

Source: Diagnostics Telephone Survey of Primary and Secondary Schools, Oct. 1997

Clearly, the main responsibility was seen to lie with pupils and subject teachers, with just under half suggesting that the parents played a major role (although almost all schools saw them as having some responsibility). Interestingly, less than 40% of schools assigned a major role to tutors. Only about half the schools commented on mentors, who were not generally seen as having a major role. What kind of role was expected of parents and mentors, in managing the homework process? As we saw in

Chapter 2, many of the primary schools we visited encouraged parents to play a very active and collaborative role, which parents generally welcomed. The telephone survey summarised the views of the larger group of schools, in relation to pupils in three year groups (Years 3, 6 and 8) and results are shown in Table 3.9. It is clear that the main role schools expected parents to play was supervisory: their responsibility was to be clear about the work to be done and to ensure it was completed in suitable conditions. It is striking how similar the results are for the three age groups. The only change for older age groups is that schools were less likely to expect parents to supervise the child; this was balanced by the expectation that parents would 'sign off' that the work had been done.

Table 3.9
Schools' Expectations of Parents in Managing Homework

Schools hope parents will….	Y3 % of schools	Y6 % of schools	Y8 % of schools
inform teacher of any problems	98	99	92
know what homework has been set	91	92	88
ensure this has been done, and sufficient time spent	91	92	91
provide a quiet room or area for homework	89	91	91
inform teacher of any achievements	90	90	68
supervise and/or work with children	81	76	65
'sign off' homework in a homework record or diary	56	64	87
provide additional resources (books, equipment)	48	53	38
N=	226	199	141

A series of single response questions

Source: Diagnostics Telephone Survey of Primary and Secondary Schools, Oct. 1997

As we have seen, there were schools which had already formalised the respective responsibilities of parents, staff and pupils in their guidelines, and these might be incorporated in some form of **contract**. One primary school headteacher in an over-subscribed school with a strong work ethos explained how he had felt the need to clarify policy to all concerned:

➡ The head teacher had a meeting with parents after the staff had revised the homework policy. He felt he needed to outline the school's aims and objectives because things had been slipping, with some homework coming in on scrappy bits of paper. He felt that parents were unsure as to what was expected. At the meeting, which was well attended, he outlined the governors' and the school's expectations, on discipline and standards of work and homework. Parents were asked to sign to show that they understood and accepted what was expected. Those that did not attend were asked to come into the school. Parents themselves confirmed that they had been left in no doubt as to their expected involvement. This was summarised in the homework policy which set out the roles of parents, class teacher and child (see Box 3.2)

One other primary school had included a contract as a response to the new homework policy document in 1996. However, although this was well received by parents at the time, the school felt it was just as important to re-iterate the approach through regular letters.

It was unusual to find the responsibilities of each group set out quite as clearly as in Box 3.2; indeed, the roles of parents as described or implied in other schools were cast in rather more collaborative terms, with parents expected to play a more active role in supporting learning. Other schools also tended to project a more active role for pupils, with the stress as much on pupil initiative as on compliance with instructions.

Contracts on homework proved a divisive issue, with other schools insisting that what mattered was the quality of the school's partnership with parents, based on good communication about all aspects of their child's development. Some suggested that translating this into a contractual format would actually damage the relationship built up through a partnership approach. In the secondary schools we visited, too, contracts were the exception: only two of the nine mentioned a contract related to homework. Both of these also had extremely clear and rigorously implemented procedures for checking compliance with homework requirements. Other schools relied on parents to support the school's homework system by ensuring that tasks were completed. Several

produced quite lengthy guidelines, summarising the whole curriculum and how homework fitted into this, so that parents had a better idea of the framework within which their pupils were working. They often looked to parents, particularly in KS3, to provide an early warning system about problems with homework, principally through comments in homework diaries.

BOX 3.2
ROLES OF PARENTS, CLASS TEACHER AND CHILD IN A VOLUNTARY AIDED PRIMARY

Role of the parents

The role of the parent is crucial if a child is to gain success from homework. To reinforce its value through positive feedback will give children the confidence to persevere and work hard and reach high standards of achievement.

Parents can assist by:

1. Providing a table, chair and a quiet place to work

2. Negotiating with the child when homework is to be done as a child's free play is important too.

3. Ensuring that outside clubs do not hamper a child's quality of work and put a child under undue pressure.

4. Checking presentation and content of all homework being returned to school and signing/dating it.

Role of the class teacher

The class teacher controls the direction of homework and the nature of the tasks undertaken.

The teacher will:

1. Provide the stimulus and content.

2. Give full and comprehensive instructions.

3. Set deadlines for completed work and ensure that deadlines are met.

4. Mark and monitor work.

5. Provide help and support.

Role of the child

1. To listen to homework instructions in class.

2. To copy down instructions for task and deadline date.

3. To ensure that homework is completed and handed in to meet the deadline.

4. To attempt all work and give of their best.

5. To inform class teacher of any difficulties.

For parents, there was another side to these responsibilities, namely that schools should fulfil their obligations, in setting and marking homework, and should also ensure that homework demands were reasonable: that is, work that could de done within the time suggested, that was clearly defined, and for which the necessary resources had been provided (or could reasonably be found at home). More generally, parents wanted schools to ensure that homework demands were 'reasonable' for their family context. To achieve this, the school needed to be informed about their pupils' home circumstances. The evidence from the case studies suggested that, even in these generally well-organised schools, not all staff felt well informed in this respect. Class teachers of KS1 children usually had a good idea because they were in frequent contact with most parents, but with older children, and in particular in secondary schools, it seemed to be more difficult for teachers to collect and use this information in their planning of homework, except where there was a major problem. All the staff interviewed were asked what proportion of their pupils might have difficulties with homework because of their home circumstances. Half or more of the schools in the telephone survey estimated that very few of their pupils (perhaps less than 10%) faced such difficulties. A small number of schools said that the problem was much greater (perhaps half or more of their pupils had difficulties at home). However, a number of teachers interviewed on school visits said they could not really give an answer about pupils' homework circumstances, suggesting that it was not a factor that affected their planning.

From the pupils' point of view, parents played an important role in managing homework. Overwhelmingly, they confirmed that the school's message had got home, in every sense: almost 90% of both KS2 and KS3 pupils who took part in the survey in case study schools agreed that '*My parents make sure that I do my homework*'. Of the KS2 pupils, only 7% said they 'often' forgot to take their homework to school (another 37% said they did so 'a few times'). Primary school pupils were the most insistent on monitoring by parents, with almost 60% 'strongly agreeing' with the statement. Although a high proportion of pupils from each phase expected parents to help with homework as well as to police the system, there was some indication from the pupil survey that, not surprisingly, the youngest pupils were the most likely to look to their parents for help.

Procedures and protocols

It is evident from what has been said above that most of the schools recognised that an effective homework programme needed to be underwritten with very clear guidance about what was required, and what would happen if requirements were not met. While they acknowledged that homework was not legally enforceable, the great majority expected all pupils to do it, and many described it as 'compulsory'. Even in schools in more challenging catchment areas, where the home circumstances of some pupils were known to be difficult, staff felt that most parents supported them in this and some went to great lengths to help pupils to complete their homework. This was a very different approach from that of a primary school where homework was not part of assessed work and was not seen as compulsory; as the head teacher put it, '*If they don't do it, that's it*'.

What most of these schools had done was to devise and implement a clearly defined set of procedures for managing the homework process and ensuring that work was properly set, explained, completed, marked and reviewed. These procedures were therefore concerned mainly with the efficiency of the system. It was implied that if the procedures were properly followed, the system would also be effective, that is, that appropriate tasks would be set and completed, thus enhancing learning, but the systems were dealing essentially with compliance rather than quality. In general, **compliance** was achieved through clear rules, backed up by incentives and sanctions.

Achieving compliance. Schools with an established and successful programme had succeeded in winning the support of staff, pupils and parents for what all recognised as a manageable programme. In these circumstances, it was taken for granted that homework would be done. For primary schools, the key features of such a system seemed to be:

● **a clear schedule**, so that everyone knew which nights each type of task would be set and the deadlines for handing work in;

● **good instructions**; tasks had been well explained, pupils had written down the instructions and could if necessary explain to their parents what the task was;

- **two-way communication with parents**, so that they knew what their child was doing and what kind of help they were expected to give; and could also let the teacher know about problems or successes; and the school could discuss developments in homework when appropriate;

- **resources for managing the process**, for example provision of plastic bags or folders for holding reading books and worksheets, planners for recording work, homework notebooks or files for written work, a box for collecting in completed work;

- **simple but effective incentives**, such as merit marks for keeping up with homework and 'good homework' assemblies or presentations.

Most primary schools stressed that what mattered more than anything else was the quality of the partnership with parents.

➡ For example at an inner-city primary school, where half the children were eligible for free school meals and a similar proportion were from ethnic minorities, including refugees living in very cramped conditions, establishing a partnership was particularly challenging. The Year 6 pupils were somewhat ambivalent about homework, with about a third recognising its importance but being unwilling to do it. However, the head felt that attitudes were changing, with KS1 parents being much more involved in their children's work; this was attributed to the efforts of KS1 teachers , who had worked hard as a team to seek out parental support in the playground, and through notes and messages.

➡ A first school had developed its homework programme over ten years. As a result of close collaboration with parents, pupils were well established in homework routines by Year 4, in a pattern that was well understood and supported by parents and staff. Parents were encouraged to accentuate the positive by only including constructive comments in home-school diaries; problems and criticisms were to be taken directly to the teacher.

Primary staff stressed the importance of making the task as clear as possible, and ensuring that it

was accurately recorded. While many had introduced homework diaries or planners, at least for older children, some schools preferred other formats, such as a homework book in which tasks were recorded and work written. One important aspect of the programme was felt to be the discipline of learning to manage a weekly schedule or, indeed, longer assignments that had to be planned and carried out over a period of weeks.

However, a few primary schools felt that pupils would be further helped in building this self-discipline if sanctions as well as incentives were clear. They had built systems with very clear requirements, as the following example shows:

➡ At a primary school with good parental support, low eligibility for free school meals and a head who had worked on a homework programme since arriving eight years ago, the system became more tightly defined as children got older. Building on active partnership with parents in KS1, KS2 children were introduced gradually to sanctions which were part of a school behavioural policy. So, when asked why they did homework, Year 6 pupils' first response was '*because of zero tolerance*'. The norm was for all children to have a daily good behaviour record, with a merit sticker for five days' good behaviour and a letter or certificate of praise for five such stickers. Non-completion of homework was described as a 'white board offence', which meant that defaulters had their names written on the class white board and lost their good behaviour mark. The headteacher said that the policy was applied flexibly in younger KS2 classes and individual difficulties investigated. Children and parents who were interviewed supported the system. It was felt to be a useful preparation for secondary school. The school saw little point in having a policy unless it was fairly and rigorously enforced. However, the head insisted that the policy suited that school's context, and might not be appropriate elsewhere; systems had to take account of local needs and priorities.

At this school, in Year 6 unfinished work had to be completed at break or lunchtime. This was a common sanction in other schools, but here too it was important to be clear why and how this was done. One school arranged a space in the hall, near the staffroom, for pupils who had difficulty in completing their work at home. This included 'defaulters', being punished for non-completion, and those needing extra support. Some pupils suggested that it might be preferable to complete homework at school because they didn't like going out to the playground. Once again, the key issue was clarity and rigour. This included keeping a homework file to monitor returns, or ensuring that diaries were regularly checked, and making the consequences of non-completion clear. In keeping with the partnership approach, some schools felt that the most appropriate response, which might also be used as a sanction, was to send reminders home. It was common, especially for younger children, to allow extra time for completion of written assignments before applying sanctions.

In secondary schools, too, there was a balance between incentives and sanctions, but by this stage most policies started from the assumption that homework was compulsory. The key features of effective systems for achieving compliance were similar to those in primary schools but with a greater emphasis on meeting explicit requirements about:

- **recording:** Homework tasks had to be clearly defined and recorded, often in a specially designed homework planner or diary; parents were expected to record that they knew what was set and that the work had been completed;

- **monitoring:** Subject teachers and/or tutors regularly monitored that diaries were properly completed; senior staff monitored that appropriate work had been set, in keeping with the schedule;

- **follow-up:** while merit marks might be given for regular performance and/or for good quality homework, more attention was usually given to sanctions for non-compliance, from informal detention through to formal complaints to parents. What mattered, as in primary schools, was clarity and rigour. Sanctions had to be clear, fair and stringently enforced. When this was achieved, it often meant that in practice they only rarely had to be invoked.

Most schools we visited used similar mechanisms to achieve compliance. They issued **diaries or planners**, they expected these to be **checked** by parents and tutors and subject teachers, and failure to complete homework was usually

punished, with an ascending scale of penalties for repeated offences. The positive aim behind these systems was to help pupils to develop self-discipline and to learn to manage their own time effectively. It is important to remember that many Year 7 entrants had apparently done little or no systematic homework before, and therefore these skills and disciplines had to be instilled from scratch. This was the thinking behind Year 7 tutorial programmes to develop personal skills in time management and study methods, although these were sometimes rather brief. It was recognised that many pupils, not just those with special needs, required continuing tuition in how to manage independent learning.

One boys' school demonstrated the importance of consistent enforcement very firmly. Teachers who implemented the system properly had very little trouble over homework, while those who failed to do so wasted a considerable amount of time chasing defaulters. Achieving compliance therefore seemed to depend more on good management than on the school context and pupil intake. Two urban schools with rather different intakes and outcomes, one in the north and one in London, had different styles but a common stress on consistency and fairness.

➡ At the northern school there was an emphasis on flexibility and positive incentives. The staff had debated the value of having a fixed homework timetable, feeling it was more appropriate to set homework as and when the need arose. But pupils and parents found this was unbalanced and difficult to monitor, and a timetable was reintroduced. A merit system helped to encourage compliance and homework was generally completed on time. Diaries were introduced and tutors were required to check them regularly; pupils' responses indicated that this was happening. The system was further monitored by the heads of year, who checked one-sixth of the diaries each half term (so that all were seen during the year). This exercise was also used to monitor how far teachers were complying with the homework timetable and the departmental policy document. If pupils regularly failed to complete homework, staff contacted their parents. The deputy head was clear that it was important to differentiate between those pupils who would not work and those whose domestic circumstances meant that they could not work. Although detention was used, particularly by some departments, as a punishment for non-completion, the deputy head was wary about this, feeling it could be counter-productive and could reinforce the notion of homework as a form of punishment. The process of clarifying and tightening up the system was still continuing.

➡ The most highly structured system for managing homework was found at the London school. This high-achieving, grant-maintained comprehensive school, which had built up its systems for an intake with a wide ability range, set very high expectations for pupils and parents. The homework system, backed by a parental contract, depended on rigorous monitoring. Much of the homework policy was taken up with the details of the system which was outlined as follows:

- Pupils wrote their homework in a homework diary

- Teacher wrote the homework into a class diary

- Parents checked and signed the homework diary

- Tutors checked and signed the homework diary

- Referral slips were issued if pupils failed to hand in their homework

- Letters were sent out to parents and slips were accumulated by the senior house master

- If four slips were accumulated, the pupil was punished.

The class homework diary, which was carried by a single pupil, enabled homework to be readily monitored (by the head among others), and after school was kept in the school foyer. If a parent wanted to know what homework had been set, they could ring the school and ask for the diary to be checked. Pupils related carefully and with some trepidation the system for tracking and following up boys who did not hand in homework, but they said that in practice this rarely happened.

Both schools mentioned the good relationships they had with their parents. As in primary schools, this seemed to be the foundation of effective

management systems. While these systems often appeared more formal in secondary schools, in keeping with the scale and complexity of the institution and the age of the pupils, the basic requirements of clarity, fairness and rigour were very similar. One school which took part in the telephone survey had summarised the requirements of an effective system (Box 3.3).

BOX 3.3
A SECONDARY SCHOOL'S CRITERIA FOR AN EFFECTIVE HOMEWORK SYSTEM

HOMEWORK SYSTEMS WORK BEST WHEN:

- a department addresses the issue of homework setting collectively and develops a homework policy

- the departmental policy is to include homeworks in the scheme of work

- setting of homework is regular, in line with the homework timetable and given priority in lesson time

- collection and checking of homework is regular, prompt and consistent

- homework is marked and returned promptly

- parents are kept informed of difficulties

- demands are realistic

- approaches to organising and completing homework are developed and supported in the tutorial programme

- the needs of children of different abilities are taken into account

- tutors support individual needs in respect of homework

- parents are informed of the homework programme and policy

Encouraging pupil self-management. Two procedural issues, relevant to either phase, merit further comment. These relate to **time management** and the use of **diaries or planners.** Some schools in each phase wanted to teach pupils to manage their own time by giving them a week or more to complete work, and expecting them to plan their schedule around their other commitments. Others felt this was unrealistic, and that it was more effective to instil the habit of regular work by regulation, ensuring that homework had to be completed within one or two days at the longest, except for occasional long assignments. One primary introduced a constrained element of time management by setting some work to be completed over a four-day period (Monday to Friday). It may be recalled from Chapter 2 that many primaries felt that it was more effective to test 'learning' homework after a week, rather than after a day or two. In secondary schools, deadlines were often dependent on the lesson timetable, work being required 'by the next lesson', possibly one week later. What mattered was that the issue of time management was explicitly discussed and the merits of, and rationale for, differing timespans and rules actively debated. One useful tactic was to record the 'date due' systematically in the homework diary, at the time work was set.

By KS4, most schools expected and indeed required pupils to manage their independent study time effectively, and guidelines issued at the beginning of the year usually discussed this. It was helpful when all the deadlines for GCSE coursework, which was the mainstay of many KS4 homework programmes, were clearly set out. The urban technology college we visited, which was working hard to make its procedures clearer and more effective, had taken other measures to help pupils to manage their own learning:

➡ Teachers gave advice, for example on how to make the best of relatively slack periods, and provided reading lists. The school had introduced a system of detailed performance monitoring, with individual targets being set in KS4. In addition to homework, voluntary Year 11 after-school lessons had been introduced, to help pupils achieve or surpass their targets - around half the year group had signed up for three hours extra tuition. For the less motivated, the school's new 'discipline for learning' system had provided the clear framework and sanctions they needed.

The widespread introduction of homework **diaries or journals** to help pupils manage their homework was one of the most striking features of the study. In the telephone survey, all the secondary schools and 70% of the primary schools gave pupils some form of homework notebook. The diaries ranged from very simple booklets, hand-written and school produced, to highly professional printed planners, with much additional information to cover most aspects of school life. There were one or two commercial versions found in many schools, sometimes customised with the school's name.

Most schools issued their diary free to pupils (with replacements often charged for) but a few expected pupils to buy it (for example, at a cost of £3.00). The issue here is how useful the documents were for supporting the homework programme. Here is the comment of an inspector visiting one of the secondary schools:

The school has introduced a 'diary and planner' to help pupils to record and plan their homework. This is a potentially useful aid with space for both a note of each homework and when it must be completed. A weakness, as with most similar documents , is the very limited space to record the nature of each homework [a space 6cm by 9cm per day] - thus details have often to be recorded somewhere else (e.g. the back of an exercise book or rough book).

In fact, this planner, in an A5 format and with two pages per week, provided rather more space than many others. Some used the second page of each two-page spread for parents' comments or other notes on achievements, while others had a much smaller format, still with a double page per week. Figure 3.5 overleaf shows how crowded entries could become, when conscientiously recorded.

A number of secondary schools used a commercial booklet with a customised school cover, while others preferred a more school-specific document with school dates and deadlines incorporated in the main pages. Figure 3.6 overleaf shows the format of a well-designed booklet of this type which includes useful school information and maximises the space for recording. One school had a commercially sponsored ring binder into which A5 advice and homework sheets could be entered. This had the advantage that sheets covering past work could be removed for monitoring, thus keeping the file reasonably slim.

Notebooks produced by and for primary schools were generally less ambitious, their main purpose being to record work set and to encourage dialogue with parents rather than to serve as a general diary and advice compendium. A number of schools were using a commercially produced A5 'homework diary' which incorporated simple advice, with a weekly double page to note 'reading', 'spelling', 'tables' and 'other work' on one side, with the other page for 'Things to remember' and parents' comments (See Figure 3.7 overleaf).

Figure 3.5
Extract from a secondary homework diary

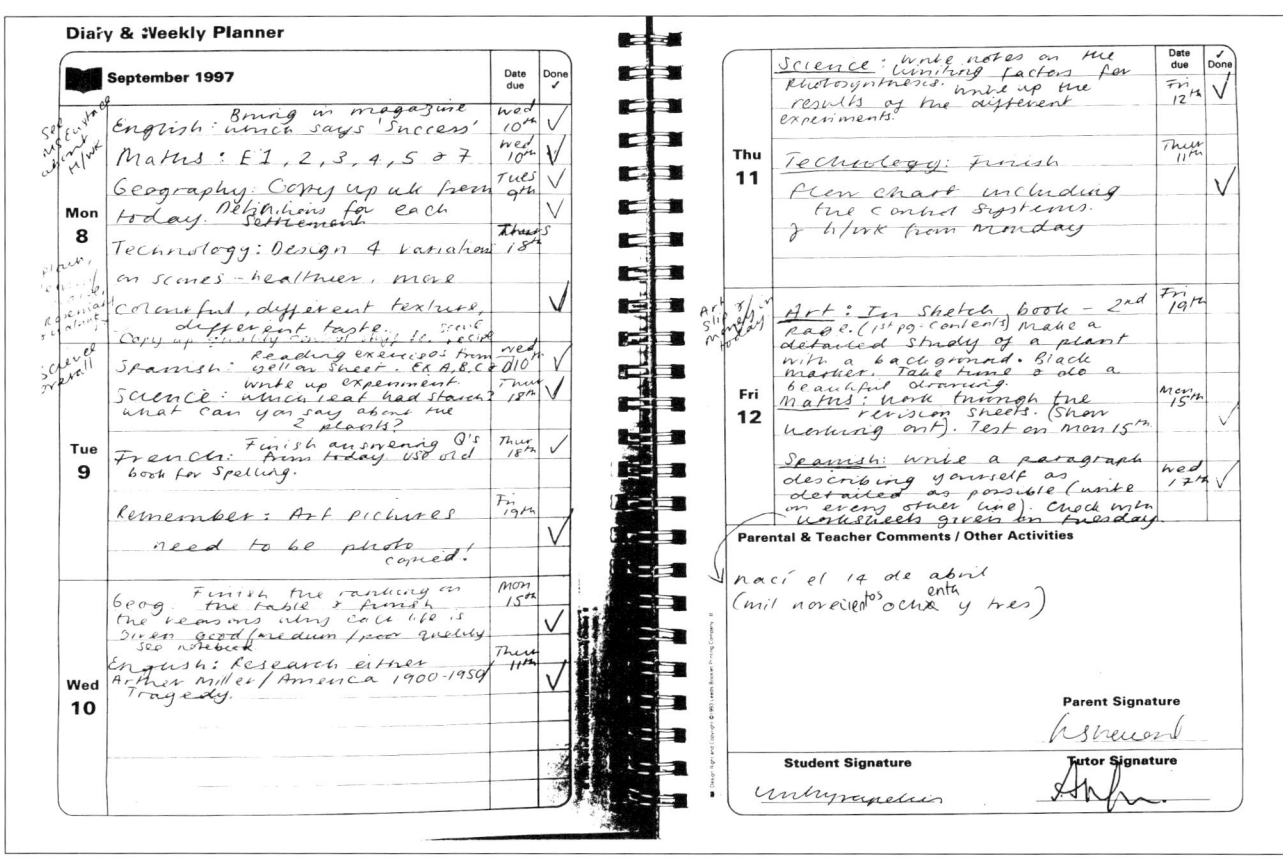

Figure 3.6
Format of a school-designed KS3 homework diary

WEEK BEGINNING September 22nd 1997

	Subject	HOMEWORK	Due in	Done ✔	Teacher Comment (if required)
Monday					
Tuesday					
Wednesday					
Thursday					
Friday					

School finishes at 1.10 pm today to allow staff time to prepare for visits by Prospective Parents this evening.

Lesson 2 - House Period

COMMENTS: Parents are invited to make comments here.

16

Parent's signature _____

15

Parents - please initial if correspondence has been received this week: ☐

Tutor's signature _____

In all, at least 12 of the 19 primary schools we visited used a homework diary or notebook, some for all pupils, others for KS2 only or perhaps just for Year 6. For younger children, home-school communication was generally maintained through the Reading Record, and homework tasks were sometimes added to this. Box 3.4 shows a page from a 'link book', introduced for KS2 pupils in one school, which combines the functions of homework notebook and reading record. Parents commented that although tasks were sometimes recorded in a rather cryptic code, they could usually work out what was required. In this school, Year 6 pupils had a homework diary in addition to the link book. Teachers in other schools, however, preferred to set out tasks on sheets which they could send home, so that they could be sure all children (and parents) had a clear guide. In almost all cases, however, the document was intended as a two-way record, with parents as much as (and sometimes more than) a record for pupils, and built on the reading diaries which were common in KS1.

In general, diaries and planners seemed to fulfil a useful function, but perhaps greater care was needed to ensure that the layout really served the intended purpose and did not create unrealistic expectations for pupils or parents (for recording targets and achievements or detailed comments). The key elements seemed to be:

- **Sufficient space to record the work set.** Most schools wanted pupils to copy down an accurate account from the board, although many preferred their own 'shorthand' version - partly because the diary space was cramped.

- **'Date due' and 'completed' boxes.** It was a useful discipline for teacher and pupil to complete this, and a box encouraged them to do so.

- **Prompts for monitoring by parent, teacher/tutor.** If each person expected to 'sign off' homework had a designated space it made the task easier for all.

- **Space for comments (by pupil, teacher, parent).** How realistic is it to expect regular comments? This can be as burdensome as completing a visitors' book. But schools and parents valued the encouragement to comment if this was needed, and primary pupils seemed to like joining the 'dialogue'.

Figure 3.7
A Year 4 diary extract

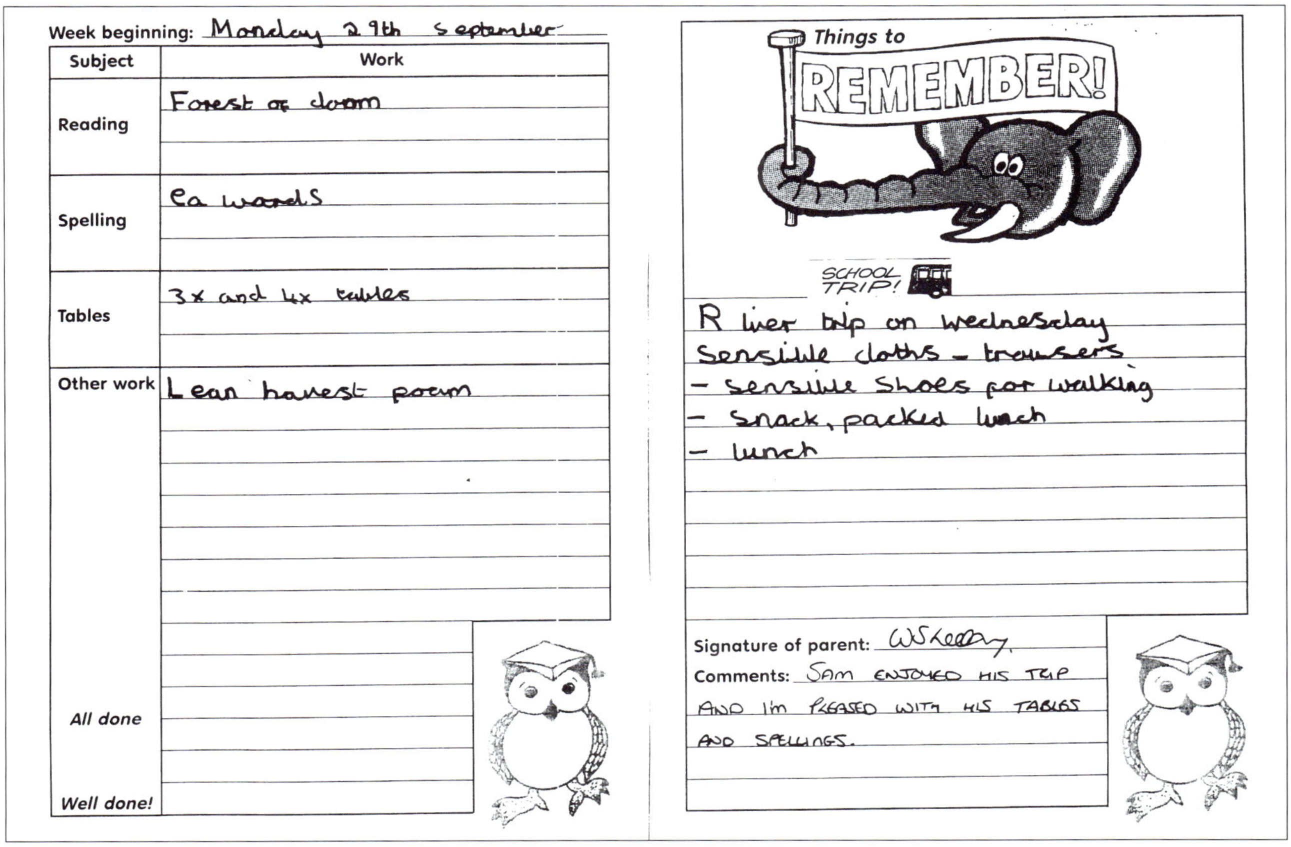

BOX 3.4
USING A LINK BOOK IN YEAR 3

The school's policy statement explained how the link book is introduced at school entry (in Nursery or Reception), as a reading record and for dialogue with parents. By Year 3, as homework increases, pupils are expected to use their link book to record their homework tasks, as well as continuing its use as a reading record. (The policy suggests reading at the front, homework at the back, but this is not the practice followed in the extract below). [Parents' comments in *italic*, child's in red]

Autumn Term 1997

3/9   **14 Rats And A Rat Catcher**

Mary read the beginning of this story to me today - no mistakes - lovely! Next time choose something a little more difficult.

4/9   **Roger was a Razer Fish**

Please read a few pages tonnight

Mary read the whole Book to me just a few mistakes

Thank you

5/9   1.   Homework mathematics sheet (mon)
      2.   5 places with miles

8/9   Homework for Thurs

      1.   Science sheet
      2.   Look at library book (ret Fri)

Dinosaur's Divorce

17/9   *Lee had a lot of help to do his work. Can we use guide lines?*

That's fine

19/9   1.   Park sheet for Monday
      2.   3 things you have found out from your libry book

Trailbikes

      1.   The Pars-Docker rally is an endurance race for motor cycles and oth vehicles
      2.   Grass track racing looks exciting
      3.   Moter bikes arefun

15/10   *Eleanor has been given the 'horrible history' book, 'The Awesome Egyptians' which has captured her imagination. She read about 1½ chapters out loud to me and had been reading it most of the evening as well, telling me about bits of it here and there.*

17/10   1. Mathematics   2. Tesco

Eleanor is probably preferring to read to herself now that she is so fluent. That's fine as long as you discuss the content and meaning.

Other useful elements included 'things to remember' boxes and a record of time spent. A number of schools had a different format or contents for each key stage, in order to make it more relevant and appropriate. Given the cost of supplying diaries to all pupils, care is needed to ensure that the layout and contents really serve the intended purpose. Most schools expected tutors to explain the use of the diary to pupils at the start of the year and to see that they were properly maintained, but there was little point in pupils (and teachers) complying with these rules unless there was evidence that the diary actually met the goal of helping pupils to manage their work effectively. It seemed as if the pupil was then seen as responsible for maintaining an accurate record, with action only being taken when deadlines were missed. Perhaps more could be done to use the diary process, as pupils get older, as the basis for more explicit teaching and development of time management skills.

3.3   Steering the Strategy

So far in this chapter we have focused on the efficient maintenance of a homework programme. However, if the programme is to fulfil its wider purpose of promoting learning, on the lines suggested in Chapter 2, then active leadership and strategic planning are required. Moreover, the strategy has to carry everyone with it - staff, pupils and parents - and this calls for a continuing effort in communication and consultation. We shall use the homework policies which most of the schools we contacted had produced, and evidence about how these policies were developed, in order to identify some of the main components of an effective and dynamic homework strategy. Two aspects which deserve separate treatment concern communication - how the policy can most effectively be put over to the different groups - and evaluation.

The policy and its purpose

The telephone survey showed that nearly all the secondary schools (96%) and over three-quarters (78%) of the primary schools had homework policies. Many of these schools sent copies of their policy, adding to the examples collected from the case study schools. These documents varied considerably in their scope and audience:

- Some were written for staff only, while others encompassed all groups.

- Some covered purposes, schedules, types of work and roles and responsibilities, while others were largely procedural.

- Some presented key ideas in simple language, in a clear layout, while others were lengthy and carefully argued.

One relevant factor was the age of the document. Schools with policies were asked when their homework policy was devised and their responses are shown in Figure 3.8.

It is apparent that primary school policies had generally been devised more recently. Their significance as a tool for strategic planning is

indicated by further analyses which showed that primary schools with a written homework policy were setting more homework on a wider range of topics and tasks, had more formal methods of assessment and used a wider range of strategies to ensure homework was completed. This link was much less clear in secondary schools, almost half of which had a policy written more than five years ago. Secondary school homework policies seemed to be accepted as an unquestioned aspect of school documentation; only 43% of schools had made any change in homework policy or practice in the previous three years, and the changes were generally procedural, rather than fundamental.

Figure 3.8
When School Homework Polices were Devised

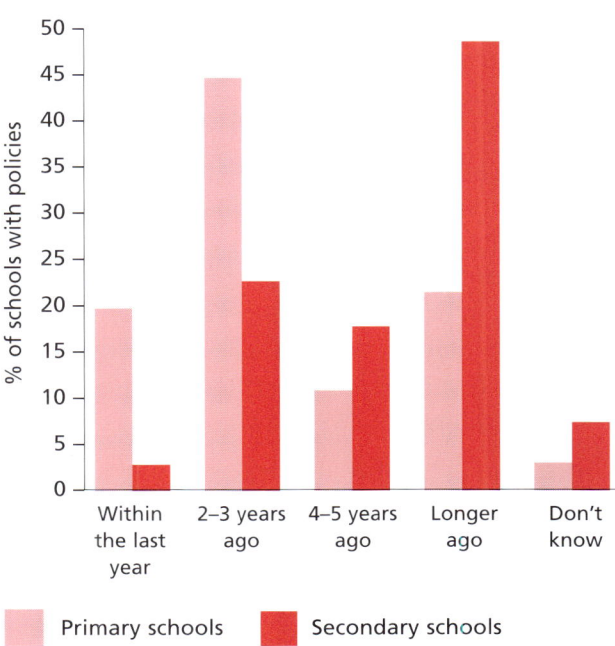

Source: Diagnostics Telephone Survey of Primary and Secondary Schools, Oct. 1997

While there can be no single formula for an effective homework policy, which must satisfy the needs and priorities of a specific school context, we can consider some questions which seem important.

How has the policy been prepared? Many of the schools, particularly the primary schools for whom homework policies were a new challenge, described how they had developed their policy. One point repeated in almost every case was that developing a worthwhile policy was a lengthy and careful process.

➡ At a primary school in a small country town, the new head had started the process on appointment in 1995. There had been some homework in place but the staff supported the decision to formalise the structure. A parents' consultation questionnaire was used to collect views on homework; the findings were discussed by the staff and the deputy head prepared a draft. The policy was trialled informally in 1996/97, amended and formally adopted by the governors' curriculum sub-committee in September 1997. A newsletter for parents explained the key issues and offered the full document if required. The policy will undergo annual evaluation from 1997/98, using feedback from parents and staff.

➡ At an inner London primary the deputy head had taken the lead in developing the policy. After wide consultation, a draft was written by the deputy and a parent governor and taken to the staff for discussion. It was then circulated to parents for comments before ratification by the governors. Practice is therefore based on a consensus view. The staff feel there is improved consistency in approach and practice, with systems in place which everyone has agreed to and understands. As the Year 6 teacher put it, *'It's really nice to have everything you believe in written down… this is what we all feel'*.

➡ The head at another semi-rural school had been at the school for twenty years but when the school became grant maintained she was keen to introduce homework in a more formal way. She used the OFSTED report on *Homework in Primary and Secondary Schools* (HMSO, 1995) as a starting point and consulted with staff on early drafts. Governors and parents were then involved before the policy was finalised.

➡ A small rural school had developed their practice gradually, as a staff team, so that homework had become embedded in the learning programme. In preparation for their OFSTED inspection they wrote down what they actually did. This had then been firmed up into a formal policy.

Whether the policy was initiated by a change of head, or grew out of established practice, whether it was meant to embody 'what everyone knows' or to work it out from first principles, the common thread was genuine consultation. The head could provide the lead, but listening to what teachers and parents really thought was an essential part of the process.

Few of the secondary policies had gone through such a development process recently, but the technology college we visited had revised theirs in the wake of their OFSTED inspection (see Box 1.1. page 12). Major overviews of a school's learning policy might provide the most appropriate stimulus for reviewing school and departmental homework policy through a thorough consultative process.

What does the policy cover? Homework policies in these and other schools covered most of the following areas:

● **Rationale** Why the school had a homework programme and how the policy had been developed.

● **Aims** A summary statement of what the school was trying to achieve through homework.

● **Practice** A description of the types of task set for homework and (in some cases) an indication of the time to be spent.

● **Consultation** How parents could be involved in the homework programme.

● **Assessment** Arrangements for marking and feedback.

● **Monitoring** How the effectiveness of the policy would be checked and evaluated, preferably with dates (when the policy was written and when it would be reviewed).

The policies were written to encapsulate the school's ethos and approach, and in some cases were aimed specifically at parents. But the audience was not always clear. Was it really written for staff (some policy documents certainly were)? Was it open to pupils? Some schools seemed to prefer a fairly short statement of principle, with the barest outline of schedule and content, reserving the details for more specific guidelines, newsletters and other forms of information to convey the gist of the policy to the different audiences of staff, parents and pupils.

In primary schools the homework policy, or guidelines based on it, could be a key document for staff, underlying and helping to promote a consistent approach. Secondary school policies needed to cover all the areas outlined above, but in practice the school policy was sometimes more of a framework document, setting out the principles on which more specific departmental policies should be based and the procedural arrangements applying to all subjects.

- A London school taking part in the telephone survey specified that departmental policies must deal with *planning, objectives, setting, types of homework (for KS3 and KS4), involvement of parents, marking, checking, assessing and monitoring*.

- The grammar school we visited specified that departmental policies should cover the following aspects:

  ○ *how students learn in their subject, and consequently what are appropriate ways of working and suitable homework tasks;*

  ○ *what are the study skills needed in their subject and how do they develop them;*

  ○ *marking and feedback, which should include a statement on how often work is marked;*

  ○ *review and evaluation of schemes of work and homework tasks;*

  ○ *sanctions for students who are not working properly.*

Some secondary school policy documents were rather bland, merely indicating that homework should be set in accordance with the homework timetable. Others focused mainly on the procedural aspects; or alternatively concentrated on principles, with little suggestion of how these might be put into practice. The challenge for secondary schools was to provide a sufficiently strong and consistent policy framework to hold together all the departmental policies within a common approach to learning, covering classroom pedagogy, assessment, study skills and resource-based learning. An alternative approach was to direct the policy document mainly towards parents, with a combination of underlying rationale, information on times and schedules and practical advice on how to help their children. In schools with a strong academic focus, cohesion could be the more readily achieved because staff and parents agreed implicitly with the need for a demanding programme of private study. Nevertheless, the documents submitted suggested that there were difficulties in meeting the needs of all the audiences and covering the procedural aspects in a single document. A more useful approach was to look for a variety of ways of translating the policy into effective practice, for all concerned.

How can the policy be put over? As several of the schools we visited made clear, drawing up a policy was only the start. Even if all the staff and some parents had been involved in its development, there was a need to continue the process of conveying the key messages, to new staff and parents and to pupils. These messages covered broadly similar ground - the why, what, where and how of homework - but were presented in different formats for different groups and purposes.

Staff. **Written statements** were an important resource for staff. In many cases the policy document was aimed at staff, often with additional guidance on scheduling, procedure, marking and types of work. Alternatively, these matters were sometimes dealt with in a separate 'staff guidelines' document, leaving the policy statement as a short summary of principles. In secondary schools, policy presentation was often devolved to departments, which had to translate the school's framework into a working strategy for their team. Here again, departmental homework policies varied from short, summary statements to carefully developed guides on every aspect of homework practice.

But staff also needed to **talk** about policy and practice. As we have seen, some primary schools involved all or most staff in the development of the homework policy, and this proved one of the most effective methods of ensuring it was known, understood and implemented. Usually the process was led by the headteacher, or another senior manager. In secondary schools, departments were often the key focus for detailed policy development. It was not easy to discover the process leading up to the writing of departmental policies, unless they had been recently produced and were part of a new initiative, such as the art homework programme discussed in Chapter 2. Here the communication process involved not just a policy statement but the development by the staff team of the whole structure of the homework programme and associated materials, which embodied the rationale and approach. In other words, conveying the policy message to staff had to be seen as a **process,** in which written statements were no more than indicators.

This process could involve:

- **Regular discussion.** Homework was just one of many topics discussed as part of team planning meetings which considered content, approach and management procedures.

- **Induction.** New staff had the school's approach explained and were given help in preparing and managing homework.

- **Review and appraisal.** Drawing on regular monitoring practice, homework became part of the appraisal agenda or was the subject of specific review by senior staff.

- **Pupils and parents.** In order to put over school policy to pupils and parents, staff prepared their own materials and 'key messages'.

The key feature of schools where staff were 'on message' about homework policy was that homework was actively and regularly on the agenda for staff discussions, at senior level, within year or subject teams, and by SEN staff. The result was evident in the consistency of staff response and practice noted on visits.

Parents. Many schools produced homework guidelines for parents, and some examples have been given in Chapter 2, to show how schools were using homework to explain and promote home-school learning. Sometimes the information was conveyed through different media such as school or class newsletters, workshops and conversations. However it was done, schools tried to cover the following aspects:

- **Policy rationale.** Reasons for and aims of homework, how it supports learning, importance of parental support and collaboration.

- **Parental role.** How to help the child, by:
  - providing appropriate conditions;
  - ensuring the task is clear;
  - working with the child where appropriate (reading, games, learning);
  - checking the time spent;
  - ensuring the work is completed and taken to school;

  - helping to find materials, articles etc.

Some guidelines also set out the school's requirements or expectations (for example weekly or daily signing/checking of diaries, sanctions procedure).

- **Scope and schedule.** At a minimum, this would summarise the quantity and timing of homework, but some offered much more:
  - homework timetable or task list, showing days when work is set and handed in where relevant;
  - suggested time allocations;
  - types of task or outline of topics;
  - advice on working with child where relevant;
  - summary of curriculum for the term or year and the place of homework in it.

Group discussions in the case study schools suggested that parents of primary children greatly appreciated information that was clear and explained the thinking behind the homework programme in a straightforward way. They found it helpful to have regular letters or outlines from the class teacher tailoring the policy to their children's programme. While little direct evidence was gathered from secondary phase parents, staff and pupil comments suggested that a clear outline of requirements was particularly important; parents liked to have a copy of the timetable, to know when work was due to be handed in and how far they were 'allowed' to help. One survey school had included relevant information in a clear and informative curriculum guide; on each subject page, the number of lessons per week and the weekly homework allocation (in minutes) were clearly set out, and the last section, headed '*HOW YOU CAN HELP*' included suggestions for how to help with homework in that subject, (e.g. testing French vocabulary and helping to rehearse role plays) and the kind of extra support that would be valuable (e.g. borrowing French books or tapes from the library, or watching natural history programmes together).

Pupils. A number of examples have already been given of how homework policies and rationale were conveyed to pupils. Some schools wrote their guidelines jointly for pupils and parents, but those which provided pupils with diaries or planners often included guidance and basic requirements. However, there were many other opportunities for teachers to put the message over. For primary class teachers, this was an ongoing daily process, backed up by senior staff. In secondary schools it required more co-ordination, within and between departments. There was an important role for tutors, both in tutorial programmes and through weekly monitoring procedures, to ensure that policy was indeed being followed by staff and understood by pupils. As we indicated above, schools with a clear and consistent policy and procedures had little difficulty in getting this across to pupils. Indeed, discussions with pupils in both KS2 and KS3 showed that they had absorbed the rationale as well as the procedures:

It helps me to get on - I want to find out how much I can do without the teacher helping.

It stops me getting bored at home.

It helps you to remember things in class.

I'd like to think it isn't important but it is because it helps you with work in school and later in life.

You do it so the teachers can find out how much you can actually concentrate and how much you can put in.

You do homework because it gets you more education, so the teacher knows how good you are and so you can organise yourself.

Where there were difficulties, it could usually be linked to inconsistent practice or a failure by staff to meet their stated or perceived obligations: for example, by setting too much routine 'finishing off' or other humdrum exercises (what one teacher called 'homework creation'); or by undue delay in marking and returning work; or by inadequate feedback. Indeed, many schools judged the efficacy of their communication by the results: that the great majority of pupils followed the procedures and handed in satisfactory work on schedule.

From policy to whole-school strategy: strategic planning, review and co-ordination

It was clear from all the schools we contacted that homework policy was accepted as a senior management responsibility, because it affected all pupils and all staff. It did not follow, however, that senior managers necessarily had a strategy which:

- linked homework policy clearly to other aspects of learning;

- planned for continuity, progression and coherence in homework, from the youngest to the oldest age groups;

- ensured the programme was manageable; and

- evaluated the school's progress towards achieving these goals.

Evidence of good practice in this area was harder to find and therefore particularly valuable.

Strategic planning. Since primary school homework programmes invariably involved core tasks in literacy and numeracy which were undertaken by all age groups, there was an obvious need to plan in progression and differentiation, so that all pupils could make progress at the right level, both within and between classes. As we saw in Chapter 2, this was often done by adopting a common approach (such as a phonics programme, a published mathematics or spelling scheme or a standard procedure for learning tables). It was less usual but all the more impressive to find example of planned progression in other tasks such as the construction of personal studies or book reviews. These schools showed they had thought well beyond simple quantitative measures (e.g. more homework for older children). Progression could also be applied to broader skills. Two first schools showed that it was possible, by careful development from Reception class onwards, to equip pupils with the skills and habits of independent learning by the end of Year 3, a time when other schools were just beginning to introduce homework.

Box 3.5 overleaf records the reflections of one experienced commentator, following a school visit, on the benefits of a whole school strategy. This is a city school with about 22% of pupils eligible for free school meals.

In secondary schools strategic planning took other forms. At whole school level, there was a clear distinction in many policies and in discussion between the type and quantity of homework set for the two key stages. Indeed, some guidelines saw KS3 homework as essentially a preparation for the

BOX 3.5
A PRIMARY SCHOOL STRATEGY

Strong leadership and a commitment to homework is an important factor in the successful implementation of the policy. A particular feature of the practice at the school are the strong systems in place for monitoring and evaluating the impact of policy and practice.

Consistency is achieved through:

- agreeing on amounts set and timings school-wide

- close monitoring to ensure that the policy is being followed

Progression is achieved through:

- regular communication with parents

- regular marking, following the school's positive marking policy

- using homework to reinforce areas of learning

Manageability is achieved through

- shared understanding and agreement about purpose

- having clear systems for communicating information and providing feedback

- planning times for homework at the beginning of each term

- building up a bank of resources to share

Purposeful homework is achieved through:

- focusing on core skills in the early stages of schooling, then broadening the base to include topic areas

- addressing a range of dimensions

- having high expectations as to quality

- valuing homework in the same way as work undertaken in class

demands of GCSE coursework in KS4, which required well-developed skills in the management of independent learning. However, it was unusual to find any provision or requirement at school level for systematic development of, or assessment of progress in, those skills through the three years of KS3. It seemed to be assumed that this was the responsibility of departments, and undoubtedly some subject teams planned for progression through homework, not only in knowledge and understanding but also in skills such as reading and information retrieval, project planning and effective revision strategies. However, since so much responsibility for the planning and management of homework was delegated to

individual subject teachers, this kind of strategic planning at school or departmental level was not the norm.

Strategic review, evaluation and co-ordination. While systems for monitoring compliance were relatively common (though not always fully effective), very few schools systematically evaluated the impact of their homework programme to discover whether, and in what ways, it was meeting the intended goals. Most schools relied on professional judgement expressed through a variety of channels. The telephone survey indicated the strategies that were most commonly used (Table 3.10).

Table 3.10
Selected Strategies for Reviewing the Impact of Homework Policy in Primary and Secondary Schools

Homework review strategy	Primary % of schools	Secondary % of schools
General review		
Ensure homework is discussed with parents	93	95
Discuss homework and its impact with pupils	89	94
Discuss homework policy in staff meetings	91	90
Annual review	5	13
Governors monitor policy	7	0
Monitoring compliance procedures		
Check diaries	6	25
Monitor that homework is set within guidelines	0	5
Specific review/evaluation strategies		
Discuss homework as part of staff appraisal	16	40
Set specific targets within school development plan	19	39
Departmental head reports back	na	22
Send questionnaire to parents	2	5
N=	227	141

Based on two questions. Items in italics are based on spontaneous responses.

Source: Diagnostics Telephone Survey of Primary and Secondary Schools, Oct. 1997

In fact, heads and deputies were first asked how they monitored homework policy generally and then whether they had carried out any specific evaluation. Their replies to the second question suggested that this was not a useful distinction for schools. The table suggests that all schools kept homework policy under review in some way, but only a minority mentioned more specific strategies to check compliance or evaluate impact. Secondary schools were more likely to incorporate homework into other systems (appraisal or school development planning), but only a minority did so. It was not clear how the achievement of homework policy targets in the school development plan was to be assessed. A very small number of schools in each phase mentioned that they were using parent questionnaires as part of their evaluation strategy. It is not easy to investigate evaluation processes from a survey of this kind, but one survey secondary school provided a very full account (Box 3.6).

BOX 3.6
SECONDARY STAFF HOMEWORK REVIEWS

The homework policy document devoted one section to homework review, setting out clearly how the review (by senior managers) would be conducted:

*Each term the Senior Management Team will undertake two homework reviews. One of these will focus on a particular **department**. The second will focus on a particular year group. The purposes of the review are to enable the SMT to:*

- *gain an insight into the range and quality of the homework set by the department;*

- *assist the department with its own ongoing evaluation and development of homework;*

- *monitor the quantity and quality of homework being set to a particular year group and provide feedback to both year teams and departments;*

- *gain an insight into how pupils across the ability range are coping with homework and provide feedback on this to both year teams and departments.*

The section presented questions for the review grouped under five headings: purpose, quality and amount of homework, coursework and responding to pupils' work, and ended with the procedure for the review. This included examination of homework done by three pupils from each teaching group involved and discussions with pupils and teachers. The process was to result in a written summary and an action plan.

The schools we visited were able to give more details about how they judged the success of their policy and any evaluation or monitoring strategies. First, it was clear that systematic procedures were most likely to be aimed at monitoring compliance, particularly in secondary schools, but could build evaluation into the process.

There were examples of this process at both primary and secondary schools:

➡ The monitoring of diaries by the heads of year at a northern secondary school was used as a comprehensive review of the quality as well as quantity of homework set and pupils' completion of the diary. In this way potential problems could be picked up. In addition, all homework policies were monitored regularly at departmental meetings and homework was discussed at monthly meetings of the pastoral support and curriculum advisory groups.

➡ At a large 11-18 GM school, implementation of the homework policy was seen as largely the responsibility of the heads of department (HoDs). All staff were expected to keep a record of lessons taught and homework set, and HoDs were expected to check these periodically. However, not all HoDs were taking their role seriously, a fact that was clear to senior managers who each line-managed a number of departments. In the current year all HoDs were being released from timetable for one week to monitor the work of their department, including homework.

➡ At an East London primary a rigorous monitoring system helped staff to assess whether or not their approach was meeting pupils' needs. A sample of home-school books was collected from each class every term to check for compliance with the policy. Written feedback was provided by the deputy on the quality of the homework set.

More commonly, however, primary schools had no formal evaluation framework, keeping developments and quality under review as a part of regular discussions. The responsibility for evaluation usually rested with the head, although this was clearer in some schools than others. For example at one inner-city primary, the head evaluated homework as part of a regular review programme; this involved a different curriculum area each week and classroom observation of individual teachers. Two schools were planning evaluations which would involve staff and possibly pupils and parents. One junior school, which reviewed homework each September in the context of NCA results, had also undertaken a survey of pupils' responses to homework, which were broadly favourable. At least one secondary school had surveyed parents, showing strong support for the homework policy.

What these examples suggest is that schools may be missing opportunities to complement their ongoing review with a more structured evaluation of homework policy, using procedures which may be at least partly in place (such as monitoring of homework diaries, observation of lessons or appraisal systems). To make such an approach effective, managers need to clarify targets or objectives which they are aiming to achieve in or through the homework policy. This may involve closer analysis of the purposes and goals of the policy itself and identification of relevant performance indicators. Deciding on specific targets to include in the school development plan may be one way of achieving this.

The procedure is likely to be more purposeful where the school has already demonstrated how homework policy fits into its overall learning development strategy, so that success criteria can be identified in terms of classroom practice and achievement. As Chapter 2 showed, it was relatively unusual for this integration to be made explicit in a school's documents beyond the level of principle, but it was easier to identify from school practice in those primary schools where the head gave a clear policy lead. In most secondary schools, where departmental policy and practice is dominant, only a major learning development initiative is likely to provide the impetus to locate homework effectively within an overall strategy.

3.4   Investing in Homework

Where senior managers had made homework a policy priority they also had to provide the human and material resources to implement that policy. This meant, for all schools, making decisions about staff time (for planning, setting and marking) and about material resources needed for the **regular homework programme**. It might also involve

decisions about extra resources, to support additional initiatives that could be seen as outside that programme: for example, to increase access to computers, to set up homework clubs for some or all pupils, or to initiate related programmes to improve independent learning.

Resourcing the regular programme

We have seen that a majority of the schools we contacted had assigned some central funds to materials in support of the homework programme:

- **Equipment.** For KS1 and some KS2 pupils this often took the form of bags or folders, sometimes including a pencil and rubber, so that work could be safely carried to and from home.

- **Diaries or home-school books** were also provided, usually free of charge. Sometimes parents were expected to buy the diary or to provide an exercise book for homework (one school sold an A5 'hard-backed book').

- **Topic outlines, class letters, curriculum guides.** A number of primary schools took considerable care to keep parents informed with regular, well produced outlines; and some secondary schools compiled curriculum guides for each year group, incorporating homework requirements.

However, the heaviest cost came from homework materials that had to be supplied to each pupil, in particular textbooks, worksheets and other consumables. For some secondary schools there was an issue about allowing textbooks home, particularly when these were used with several classes. At least three of the secondary schools we visited mentioned this could be difficult, and one of them did not generally provide pupils with personal copies of textbooks in any subject. Much use was consequently made of photocopied worksheets.

An overview of the resources which schools provided was obtained from the telephone survey (Table 3.11). The table suggests that most of these schools felt they had relatively few problems in providing the necessary resources, for any year group (most schools said there was no year-group difference in the resources supplied). It must be remembered that these were all schools identified by OFSTED for the quality of their homework practice, which may help to explain this rather positive finding. Certainly, public concern about shortages of textbooks was not borne out in this survey; almost two-thirds of schools in each phase indicated that pupils could retain reading books or textbooks until the work needed to be handed in, in sharp contrast with the schools surveyed by Johnson (1997).

Pupils themselves (in the case study schools, selected for their good practice) felt that they were not usually short of resources, most of which were supplied by school (Table 3.12). The great majority (over 80%) in each group were supplied with worksheets and almost as many KS3 pupils said they had textbooks which they could take home. KS2 pupils were much less likely to have textbooks (just under a third did so), but this low usage almost certainly reflected the type of tasks set at that stage which seldom involved the use of textbooks. One interesting finding from the pupil survey is the proportion of pupils who had access to a computer at home: almost half the KS2 pupils and over half (57%) of KS3.

Table 3.11
Resources which Pupils could take Home, KS2 and KS3

Resources supplied for homework	Y3 % of schools	Y6 % of schools	Y8 % of schools	Y10 % of schools
Exercise books or folders for their work	89	94	94	97
Textbooks, reading books or other printed material	96	98	91	96
Photocopied extracts, worksheets for individual use	94	98	94	98
Other materials (e.g. small equipment, craft materials)	38	44	72	78
Portable computers/ organisers for use at home	4	5	26	28
Access to computers at school	na	na	12	14
Videos, tapes, cassettes, CDs	na	na	6	8
N=	226	199	141	141

Several answers could be given. Items in italics were suggested by respondents

Source: Diagnostics Telephone Survey of Primary and Secondary Schools, Oct. 1997

If an estimate is made, based on data from both surveys, of additional computer access either provided at school or on a loan basis, it might be inferred that as many as three-quarters of KS3 pupils would have some computer access for homework. Of course, access might be constrained to certain times or for certain activities, but this evidence suggests that the time is approaching when homework based on computer use might be planned, as long as access could be guaranteed for all pupils. Even in primary schools, using a computer for homework was becoming common (with the need for safeguards over the indiscriminate use of published material). One school allowed pupils to book time on its five computers, with priority being given to children without a computer at home. All the pupils were provided with their own disks.

Table 3.12
Pupils' Reported Access to Homework Resources

Resources and materials used to help with homework	Primary % of pupils	Secondary % of pupils
Worksheets prepared by your teacher	86	83
Books at home that are useful for homework	80	82
An encyclopaedia at home	62	75
A computer at home	48	57
School library books you can take home	46	67
School textbooks you can take home	32	81
A computer you can borrow from school	4	12
Did not respond to any item	1	1
N=	617	386

More than one answer could be given so percentages do not sum to 100
A total of 610 primary and 383 secondary pupils gave at least one response to this question

Source: OFSTED KS2/KS3 Pupil Survey, Autumn 1997

The pupil results also suggest that they expected to draw on their own home-based resources, particularly books and encyclopaedias (judging by pupil comments, many of these were in CD ROM format). Many schools encouraged pupils to use what they had at home, but some, conscious of equal opportunities issues, strove to ensure that all necessary resources had been provided by the school. However, pupils could be encouraged to use or supply everyday materials and articles (for example to test magnets or to practise weighing and measuring).

These findings suggest that in the 'good practice' schools included in this study, homework was not unduly constrained by shortages of textbooks, library books or other learning resources. But cautionary notes are needed. First, we have seen that at least one of the case study secondary schools did not allow textbooks to be taken home at all, and others were concerned about giving access to books. Teachers' response was to set homework within these constraints, and to encourage pupils to work in and use the school library or resource centre. Second, the research for the Educational Publishing Council (Lambert, 1997, Johnson, 1997), reviewed in Chapter 2, suggested that in most subjects school books were rarely allowed home in KS3; moreover, there was some evidence from a pilot study of geography teachers (Lambert, op. cit.) that pupils might not be well prepared to use textbooks systematically, either in class or at home. This last issue was not pursued in our study, but is one that needs to be investigated if schools are going to get the intended return on supplying pupils with books.

The alternative to supplying textbooks was to photocopy printed material. For schools themselves, there were certainly concerns about the cost and effort of photocopying, which had grown for primary schools as homework had expanded, but the greatest challenge was the amount of time taken in preparing homework materials of all kinds. Extra preparation might be required for differentiation. For example a Year 6 teacher spent a considerable time photocopying, since each child was working at a different level and needed at least three mathematics worksheets for homework. As with any teaching resources, more time was needed when the materials were teacher-generated. Many primary schools felt it was worth investing in good quality, published photocopiable materials, for mathematics, spelling and literacy tasks. Headteachers generally felt that time invested in planning homework and preparing materials was time well spent, so long as the tasks were complementing and enhancing the children's learning programme. For parents, what mattered was the quality of the material which the school provided; the most unsatisfactory situation was when a child brought home

photocopied materials that were unclear or inappropriate for the task.

The other, major component of teacher investment was in time for reviewing and assessing homework (see also 2.4). As a time management issue this was more problematic for secondary teachers, with many classes to teach and all requiring homework. Indeed, many primary teachers found it difficult to separate out time spent on marking from all their other tasks.

➦ In a London primary the extra time spent on homework by teachers only became evident with older pupils. Year 5 teachers estimated they spent two hours a week on marking, Year 6 teachers two and a half. In addition, there was the time spent on planning (about 30 minutes out of the total of three hours spent on planning a week). As one said, '*It is time-consuming to ensure that homework set is a valid piece of work*'. But they all felt it was worthwhile.

Teachers of KS1 pupils often reviewed the work with individuals in class, or assessed it through tests. It was only the more formal written tasks set in KS2 that required detailed review and marking. This could be a lengthy task. The head of the small primary with a book review programme estimated that it took him 30-40 hours a month to prepare and mark his Year 5/6 pupils' reviews, on top of an almost full teaching commitment and his other duties as a head, indicating a high level of dedication. But this was probably above average, and a different type of challenge from the regular accumulation of assessments familiar to most secondary subject teachers

There was little indication from interviews or school documents of any explicit discussion of what might constitute a 'reasonable' upper limit for hours spent on marking per week and, as we saw in 2.4, estimates of how much time teachers actually spent varied widely. However, some schools and departments had addressed the problem by recommending selective marking strategies, on the principle, 'work smarter, not longer'. Some departments had found that investing time in careful planning could also pay off, both by ensuring that prepared assignments were available for some time ahead and by pre-specifying an assessment scheme which speeded up marking. It was also possible for some staff to be given the task of developing a bank of assignments of this kind for the whole department to draw on. Most senior managers were well aware of the pressure on staff, and sought to make the time requirement manageable.

Developing additional homework-related initiatives

Another way of investing in homework, in addition to the regular programme and increasing the value which pupils could derive from out-of-classroom learning, was to provide facilities and support for doing 'homework' at school or to encourage pupils to use community-based 'homework clubs' or other facilities. The White Paper *Excellence in Schools* (1997) had stressed the value of study support, defined as 'activity outside normal lessons which helps pupils to reach higher standards', and included homework clubs of all kinds as a form of study support. Such provision is also discussed in more detail in *Extending Opportunity: a national framework for study support* (DfEE, 1998). Our investigation showed that there were many options and, indeed, some rather differing rationales for promoting alternative homework provision, or indeed choosing to encourage learning not defined as homework. We shall consider these reasons first, before reviewing the types of provision on offer and the benefits and challenges associated with them.

First, it should be said that the majority of the primary schools we visited had many questions about any provision which short-circuited the parental support and involvement which they saw as the driving force of their homework programme. Most simply said that any alternative provision was 'not needed'; indeed, one school had evidence from a parental survey to demonstrate this. Others explained why they did not want to go down this route:

➡ At a primary school with 32% of children eligible for free school meals, the head expressed his views strongly. The idea of a homework club had been discussed by staff, but the head thought it was not appropriate in the context of his school. He felt that a lot of goodwill would be lost and that it would amount to handing over responsibility for homework to the school rather than helping to develop a partnership. He preferred to work on developing parental support and involvement.

➡ The head of another primary school which had worked hard on its partnership with parents felt that there were other priorities. It was more important to invest any extra effort into working directly with parents (in this case, by setting up reading workshops particularly targeted at parents who found it hard to offer constructive help). Teachers helped pupils with difficulties at home by offering extra help during the school day. Any extra provision at the end of the day was extra-curricular (music, games etc.)

➡ The head of a junior school had no plans to introduce a homework club because he could not see a need. But he had recently sent out a letter supporting a 'Club' sponsored by the LEA - really a home learning programme costing parents £10 a year, and including videos, magazines and games, all designed to support the primary curriculum.

Where schools had 'won parents' hearts and minds', they were satisfied that this was better than a homework club at school; one such school had decided to drop their club, which they initially thought would complement other strategies, because support had quickly dwindled.

However, there were a few primaries and a number of secondaries who saw value in providing facilities for pupils to do homework at school. There were a number of reasons, with differing implications:

To compensate for home constraints. Schools were aware, although often not systematically, that there were pupils who would have problems with homework because of cramped living space or family problems. They wanted to offer the 'suitable conditions' which most parents were expected and willing to provide.

To compensate for lack of parental support. Shortcomings in homework were most commonly attributed to lack of parental support. Some parents were seen to be unwilling to help, others as willing but disadvantaged - because of pressures in their own lives or lack of English or adequate education. Some schools felt that it was fairer to the pupils to provide adult support in other ways.

To support pupils with special educational needs. Although most primary schools insisted that for these pupils parental help was essential for all age groups, help might also be given in school. Secondary schools were more likely to see the need for extra support at school, especially where the learning support department found collaboration with subject departments problematic.

To target help for certain pupils. In addition to pupils with SEN, there were other pupils seen to need help or guidance. They included defaulters and those who asked for help in particular subjects.

To give access to school resources. Schools were keen to give access to library and computing facilities, both for those in some of the groups above and for extension work, for any who wished it.

To provide extra help with revision. Revision clinics and tutorial sessions were more common in KS4 but were sometimes offered on a short-term basis for other age groups.

The resources and facilities offered showed that all these factors were certainly seen as relevant in some contexts, but there were problems about identifying and meeting needs. These went back to debates about the purpose of homework. If - as many primary schools saw it - the purpose of homework, for all but the oldest pupils, was to complement the teachers' input by involving parents more closely in their children's learning, then no extra school-based provision for pupils could properly meet this goal. But if the main emphasis was on securing extra, effective independent learning time, then school-based support was a valid alternative to parental support if (for whatever reason) the latter was not forthcoming. There was also a dilemma about which pupils should be targeted: those with learning difficulties and/or home constraints, those failing to meet homework requirements or those keen to exploit any resources the school might offer. Some schools found there was a stigma attached (by pupils) to homework support at school, which was thought to be aimed at the less than competent. Not surprisingly, provision was more acceptable in schools where it was explicitly backed by senior management and where the rationale was clear.

The telephone survey illustrated some of these difficulties and the lack of clarity there is generally about what 'alternative facilities for homework' might include. First, there was a major difference in provision between primary and secondary schools. Only 12% of primary schools said they provided any alternative facilities for doing homework, compared with 81% of secondary schools. However, more detailed responses showed that the contrast was partly a matter of interpretation. The few primary schools responding mentioned mainly homework clubs at school, at the public library or youth centre. By contrast, secondary schools referred to all the facilities available to pupils during the school day, particularly the school library and access to computers, as well as to homework clubs. One-third of all secondary schools mentioned some type of homework club, ranging from school holiday projects, through special clubs for children with SEN, to more general references to lunch-time or after school clubs. A number of schools provided some kind of after-school facility, sometimes in the form of access (to computers, library facilities or quiet space) and rather less often to help from teachers.

Schools were also asked in the survey to identify the benefits and challenges they associated with alternative homework provision. The benefits echoed the reasons suggested above, with the three main ones being shown in Table 3.13.

Table 3.13
Three Main Perceived Benefits of Alternative Homework Provision

	Primary schools % of schools	Secondary schools % of schools	
		With club	No club
Additional support from teachers	20	41	34
Access to facilities/resources	21	35	37
Good environment for learning	21	31	20
No benefits	11	0	1
N	227	51	90

Source: Diagnostics Telephone Survey of Primary and Secondary Schools, Oct. 1997

Interestingly, experience of running a club seemed to suggest that it was the additional teaching support that was particularly valued, with 41% of secondary schools with a club of some kind putting this forward. But there was a fair consensus between the phases that these three benefits - support, access to facilities and an environment conducive to learning - were the ones that mattered most. Some secondary staff added that there was a motivational strand: an effective homework club helped to create a culture of achievement, countering the idea that study was 'uncool'.

The few examples of alternative provision in the primary schools we visited drew on several of the factors mentioned above.

➡ One primary school mentioned a 'SATs Club' run for Year 6 over five weeks in the summer term. In 1997 all the children had come for the one-hour session each week and it was described by the head as 'high quality learning time', involving several subject specialists.

➡ Another (inner city) school had set up an after-school club in order to help KS2 pupils with various kinds of difficulty at home. But the pupils targeted were generally not allowed to stay on by their parents. As a result, the club had changed into a 'high status' facility with a waiting list, supported by the more committed parents and offering their children additional access to computers and the school library. There was thought to be a risk that some parents might treat it as a 'baby sitting club'.

Two schools were planning to start a club, to help those with difficulties. In one case, there was a club in a local public library, but children did not use it because it meant crossing busy roads. In the other, the head thought he would run it himself, and use it to help Year 6 pupils to make progress towards individual targets, as part of the school's developing programme of target-setting. In this way, he felt, he could focus in on problems. His approach, essentially offering extra tuition and support in school for those who needed it, was echoed by other schools which distinguished clearly between extra help from teachers during the school day and homework, which by definition (from their perspective) was work at home with parental supervision and/or support. Thus help might be given to pupils with special educational needs, before school or during lunch-time, and often included a whole range of other forms of support on offer to all, from volunteers to hear reading through clubs and one-to-one sessions offered by class teachers.

Secondary schools we visited, like those in the telephone survey, generally offered help during the school day to various groups, sometimes on a fairly informal basis. In several cases, support was offered by subject departments, without any overall framework. However, one important issue was the apparent difficulty schools had in identifying how many pupils needed such provision because they had problems in working at home. In most schools, only a small number of pupils were thought to be affected, as this report from one large comprehensive school suggests:

➡ It was reported at one urban school in the north that there were some pupils whose domestic circumstances had an impact on their ability to complete homework or to work quietly on their own. There were also pupils, particularly among ethnic minority groups, who were employed in the evenings and who did not therefore have time to do school work at home. The school had no systematic ways of dealing with this, each subject department tending to adopt a different approach. But the problem was not thought to be large enough to have a major impact on the school.

Some teachers claimed that there was a designated homework room for private study. The SENCO encouraged pupils with SEN to use the room. In addition, the mathematics department had 'mathematics hospitals', with the head of department offering an 'open door' before registration (mainly for older pupils) and lunch-time workshops where pupils could work on their own or seek help; more substantial difficulties were dealt with after school.

At another school with a sizeable minority of pupils from areas affected by social deprivation, senior staff were actively considering the possibility of setting up a homework club. Meanwhile, provision was more piecemeal:

➡ Subject departments already had long-standing arrangements for supervising pupils wishing to complete homework during lunch-time and after school, with some staff putting in a good deal of time in support. The SEN room was open from 8.10 am for pupils needing help with homework. Many children chose to work in the school library, but they were not necessarily those with difficult home circumstances. One problem in setting up any regular club was that many of the children had to catch buses home straight after school.

A technology college felt that a range of support options was appropriate and effective:

➡ The Open Learning Centre was open every evening after school for pupils to use as a base for homework or other studies. In addition there were specific groups with teacher support. There was a Year 7 homework club every Friday. An English homework club ran every Thursday for all year groups and was staffed by two teachers. The mathematics department had its three computer rooms open every evening with members of staff available. There was also a homework club once a week for SEN pupils. It was not clear, on the visit, how well subscribed these facilities were.

Only one of the secondary schools we visited had a regular, daily supervised homework club open to all pupils. It was estimated that 30-60 pupils attended, with some being 'guided' to it if they were struggling with deadlines. Another school, with a twice-weekly lunch-time club, found that pupils did see some stigma attached to it, despite the school's best intentions.

The problem of 'bussing' was mentioned by a number of schools as an obstacle to setting up an after-school club. However, this could be overcome by provision during the day, if other challenges could be addressed. As the telephone survey showed, these were mainly linked to staffing: staff who were already spending a considerable number of hours on setting and marking homework were understandably reluctant to commit themselves to further duties (although some individuals were already heavily involved). Some secondary schools also felt that there would be little pupil demand. However, a leaflet from a northern comprehensive in an urban area, sent in response to the survey, suggested that a school could set up an 'open' study centre with apparent success (although no evidence on attendance was supplied):

We operate during term time on Monday, Tuesday, Wednesday and Thursday evenings from 3.45 until 7.15pm. Membership is free to all students between the ages of 10 and 25 years. To join all you have to do is come along during 'open hours', and tell us what homework you are doing. All the facilities of the Resource Centre are at your disposal. The computers, printers and photocopies are FREE; the whole of the Library is available for research into any of your homework projects and just as important, G..., H..., S... and S... are there to help, advise and support you with any problems you may have.

The picture coming through from the schools in the study was that systematic provision for pupils to carry out their homework at school was unusual in schools deemed to have high quality homework programmes, although many schools - particularly secondary schools - were anxious to encourage pupils to use computing and library facilities 'out of hours' where this was feasible. In addition, there was a considerable amount of help on offer to pupils from dedicated teachers quite prepared to provide tuition out of lesson time. The evidence suggests a number of barriers to a more systematic approach:

Staff resources. Senior managers were often reluctant to embark on a plan which would make additional demands on hard-pressed staff, preferring to leave the initiative with those teachers who chose to offer their help to pupils.

Practical constraints. By far the commonest was transport: before or after-school clubs were not seen as feasible in schools where most pupils were bussed in. But some schools also indicated that it would be difficult to find suitable rooms.

Information. It seemed to be difficult for most schools to share accurate information about home contexts, the factors that might make it difficult for them to do their work at home and how pupils actually approached their work (including the time they spent on it). Without this kind of information, it was hard to identify needs and plan provision to meet them.

Rationale. What would be the aim of the provision and who was it for? Was it an alternative venue (for those without a suitable study environment at home)? Or a supported study context (for those unable to complete work on their own)? Or a resource-based learning facility (for anyone, but especially those who wanted to enrich their work)? Or a 'sin bin' for homework defaulters? It was difficult to provide for all these possibly conflicting needs through one strategy.

Skill development. The majority of pupils were clearly able to fulfil the homework requirements and had therefore presumably developed the necessary study and time management skills, with the support of their parents. But these skills were fostered in school in a variety of ways, through classroom practice and special programmes. It was relatively unusual for anyone to be given the responsibility for co-ordinating personal/study skill development, or to plan homework clubs and other alternative provision as part of such a programme.

Perhaps the apparent difficulty in taking a systematic approach to alternative homework provision was linked with issues about the purpose of homework. We have seen that many primary schools preferred to invest all their staff resources in partnership initiatives with parents. In secondary schools, the pupil's need for appropriate study conditions was the priority, whether these were found at home, at school or at some other study centre. But the delegation of the details of homework policy, purpose and practice to subject departments meant that in most schools it was more difficult to develop a school-wide scheme for alternative provision, to meet the whole range of needs. What was needed to drive this forward was a common approach to the development of skills needed for effective independent study.

With the publication of the new national framework in *Extending Opportunity* (DfEE, 1998), guidelines have been provided for developing such an approach to the wider issue of study support, which the document describes in this way:

Study support is, accordingly, an inclusive term, embracing many activities - with many names and many guises. Its purpose is to improve young people's motivation, build their self-esteem and help them to become more effective learners. Above all, it is to raise achievement.

The framework stresses that while study support embraces many different activities, there are a number of universal principles of good practice. For example, provision of study support facilities should form part of the strategic plans of the school if it is to secure the commitment of the senior management team and, where appropriate, partnerships with local business, community or voluntary services should be encouraged. The guidelines apply to both primary and secondary schools.

The range of study support provision envisaged in the framework might include homework clubs, holiday or after-school revision sessions and other activities linked to the curriculum. It is stressed that study support is seen to be beneficial not only for pupils but also as a means of supporting teachers by involving other partners, including parents, in the process and of offering them a new opportunity for professional development.

On the face of it, an initiative of this kind seems to address different priorities from those relevant to a regular, 'compulsory' homework programme; as the definition of study support makes clear, attendance at study support activities is voluntary. However, it highlights the importance of clarifying the purpose behind homework requirements and the learning goals which homework is intended to promote. It also draws attention to the value of needs analysis; that is, of listening to what pupils say about what helps them to work well and the factors which get in the way of effective learning. If homework is such an important component of the overall learning programme, then this type of analysis seems essential to its success, especially for pupils who, for whatever reason, find independent study the greatest challenge.

3.5 Overview: The Well-Managed Homework Programme

In this chapter we have been considering how schools manage their homework programme, and what is needed to manage it effectively. We have seen that schools develop quite complex systems for implementing their homework programme. These include time allocations and schedules, to provide a fair balance of work for pupils and teachers, and rules for setting and explaining tasks, for collecting and returning work and for recording work set and completed. Linked to these systems are procedures to ensure compliance; that is, to see that the systems are properly implemented and the rules followed, with (in some cases) detailed sanctions flow-charts. Primary school procedures may appear more informal, but this is partly because the class teacher manages most of the day-to-day process. Parents and pupils generally welcome a clear system, so that they know what is expected and when.

What has also emerged, however, is the need to set these procedures within an explanatory framework which explains why homework matters and how it contributes to learning. This may be summarised in the homework policy, but if the explanation is to be effective it has to be actively shared with all the participants - pupils, teachers and parents - in ways that will engage their commitment to homework. Schools which have recently developed or reviewed their homework policy found that bringing staff and parents into the deliberation made the policy more accessible and acceptable.

The importance of winning assent of all groups to homework policy reflects an underlying dilemma for managers: homework is essentially a voluntary activity, carried out by pupils mostly in time over which schools have no control; and yet schools want to ensure that all pupils have an equal chance to do their homework well, because they believe this is an essential element of their learning. Policies and procedures in many secondary schools suggest that in practice homework is 'compulsory'; one document even suggested that persistent failure to do it would be grounds for suspension. Primaries often preferred an outwardly softer approach, not least because responsibility for seeing homework was completed lay more with parents than with pupils - especially for younger children. They first had to be sure of parental trust and commitment.

Schools were best placed to win this commitment, from all groups, when homework was shown to have a clear place within an overall learning strategy which was firmly led by senior staff, with the backing and support of the staff team. Otherwise, it could appear as if all the effort was going into systems maintenance, with few questions being asked about the quality of the work set or how it promoted learning. A clear

strategic lead was needed because there were difficult balances to be struck and maintained if the programme was to achieve its goals. For example pupils were entitled to well-defined tasks, appropriate resources and educationally useful feedback; but this involved a heavy investment of staff time, and the programme had to be manageable for teachers. Again, if homework was an educational good, all pupils were entitled to equal access, but how were schools to manage this, since it related to family circumstances outside their control? Even providing alternative 'homework' facilities in school could increase rather than reduce the disparities, if they were taken up more by well-supported pupils than those for whom they had been mainly intended.

It seems clear, therefore, that programme management needs to be firmly linked to and informed by underlying goals and purposes. This is most evident in the area of monitoring and evaluation. Of course it is essential to see the system is functioning efficiently; but it is also important to assess how well it is meeting the educational goals set out in the policy and, indeed, to review whether these goals still meet the needs of the overall learning strategy. Systematic evaluation of the educational effectiveness of the homework programme was still proving a challenge in many schools.

INDICATORS OF GOOD PRACTICE

Primary Schools

Giving a lead

- Homework policy is led and co-ordinated by a senior manager.

- Staff and parents are actively involved in all aspects of the programme.

Developing and disseminating policy

- There is a written policy, developed consensually with staff and parents; the consultation process has taken time and reflected the local and school context.

- A range of approaches is used to continue to convey the ideas in the policy, including guidelines for pupils and parents, workshops and newsletters.

Managing time

- Homework allocations are clearly set out, probably in the form of a weekly and termly schedule setting out what work is due and when, and indicating an estimated time for tasks.

- Homework is structured to help pupils (with parental support) to develop regular study patterns they can manage.

Motivating pupils

- Pupils are encouraged to complete their work by regular feedback, praise and rewards for effort.

- Requirements are made clear to parents, and their support is enlisted so that homework is completed.

- Sanctions for non-completion are clear, but seldom need to be enforced.

- Failure to do homework is investigated before sanctions are applied.

Providing resources

- The school supports teachers by providing commercial resources or time and materials to prepare resources.

- Opportunities are taken to offer pupils additional resources where possible, e.g. access to computers or library books.

Reviewing performance

- Learning goals are defined for homework and teachers evaluate whether the tasks set are meeting these goals.

- There are systematic procedures for monitoring how programme requirements are being fulfilled (by staff and pupils), and how the programme meets their needs.

- The policy itself is regularly and fully reviewed against school development goals.

INDICATORS OF GOOD PRACTICE

Secondary Schools

Giving a lead

- Homework policy is led and co-ordinated by a senior manager.

- Other managers share the responsibility of planning and review.

Developing and disseminating policy

- There is a written whole-school policy, with common criteria for department policies.

- A range of approaches is used to continue to convey the ideas in the policy, including guidelines for staff, pupils and parents.

Managing time

- Homework allocations are clearly set out, probably in a homework timetable which is clear to parents and pupils and adhered to by staff.

- Deadlines for completing tasks are explicit and manageable.

- Homework is structured to help pupils to develop regular study patterns they can manage.

Motivating pupils

- Pupils are encouraged to complete their work by regular feedback, praise and rewards for effort.

- Requirements are made clear to parents, and their support is enlisted so that homework is completed.

- Sanctions for non-completion are clear and consistent, but seldom need to be enforced.

- Failure to do homework is investigated before sanctions are applied.

Providing resources

- The school enables staff to buy or prepare appropriate resources.

- Opportunities are taken to offer pupils additional resources where possible, e.g. access to computers or the resource centre.

Reviewing performance

- Learning goals are defined for homework and teachers evaluate whether the tasks set are meeting these goals.

- There are systematic procedures for monitoring how programme requirements are being fulfilled (by staff and pupils), and how the programme meets their needs.

- The policy itself is regularly and fully reviewed against school development goals.

4 Homework Matters: Impact on Pupils, Parents and Teachers

In the previous three chapters we have looked at schools' approaches to homework: the purposes and status they define for it, the way they use it to promote learning and the procedures they devise to manage it effectively. In this final chapter we will consider the impact of this school practice. First, we look at its implications for the pupils themselves, particularly those we talked to and surveyed in KS2 and KS3, and discuss parents' views, as well as teachers' perceptions on the home context (4.1). Second, we review teachers' judgements about the impact of homework on learning (4.2). There is a short overview (4.3) of these findings.

4.1 Perspectives on Practice: Pupils and Parents

Pupils: approach, challenges, evaluation

We have seen in earlier chapters that evidence from the pupil survey, the telephone survey and visits to schools all suggested that where schools had made their homework policy clear, and the systems for setting and managing the homework process were systematically implemented, pupils readily accepted homework as a natural and indeed inevitable part of their daily or weekly programme. Here we want to look more closely at how pupils tackled their work, especially where they did it and who helped them. How did the pattern change as pupils got older, and were there any systematic differences, between girls and boys, or pupils from different types of home background, in their approach or attitudes to homework?

Pupils were asked in the survey where they did their homework. The response was clear: the great majority, of all ages, 'usually' did it at home. Table 4.1 gives the details for primary and secondary pupils. The main difference between the two groups was that primary pupils were more likely to work at home 'with someone else'. Even those who usually worked on their own 'sometimes' worked with other people. In these schools, only a very few

Table 4.1
Pupils' reports on where they did their homework: KS2/KS3

Where homework was done	KS2		KS3	
	Usually % of pupils	Sometimes % of pupils	Usually % of pupils	Sometimes % of pupils
At home, on my own	51	32	72	22
At home, with other people	37	45	27	47
At another house	4	37	4	42
At school	2	18	2	45
At the library or homework club	2	16	2	37
On the way to or from school	1	5	1	10
N=	617		386	

A series of single response items
To simplify presentation, 'never' and 'no response' categories have been omitted
All respondents answered at least one item in this question

Source: OFSTED KS2/KS3 Pupil Survey, Autumn 1997

pupils, in either phase, usually did their homework at school, although the proportion who 'sometimes' did so more than doubled from KS2 to KS3. By then more than a third said they sometimes worked at the library or a homework club.

Figure 4.1
Whether homework was 'usually' or 'sometimes' done 'at home on my own': by year group

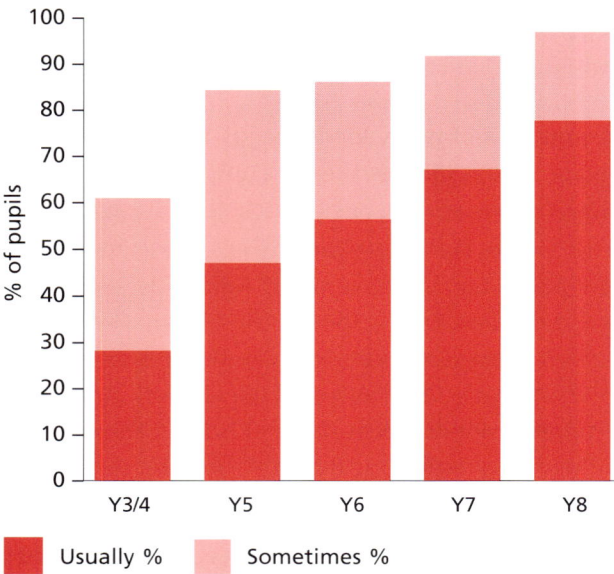

Ns= Y3/4:86; Y5:103; Y6:426; Y7:195; Y8:191

Source: OFSTED KS2/KS3 Pupil Survey, Autumn 1997

Figure 4.1 shows how the tendency to work 'at home, on my own' increased with age, from Year 3 onwards. Whereas in Year 3/Year 4 less than a third said they usually worked in this way (compared with over half who worked at home with other people), by Year 8 over three-quarters (77%) did so. This finding fits well with schools' expectations for a growing independence in tackling homework as pupils moved through KS2 and KS3. However, it is worth noticing that, in these 'good practice' schools, the development is fairly steady; there is no abrupt change between the end of primary, in Year 6, and the beginning of secondary in Year 7. In other words, it seemed that these primary schools were indeed helping pupils to become more independent, by giving them clear guidelines and helping them and their parents to understand how even open-ended tasks could be effectively tackled independently at home.

By contrast, some secondary schools were concerned that many parents who had not had the benefit of this partnership approach to homework

while their children were in primary school - indeed, whose children may not have been expected to do regular homework - needed help in understanding how to support their children appropriately.

Figure 4.2
Percentage of pupils agreeing that they worked better at home, on their own: by year group

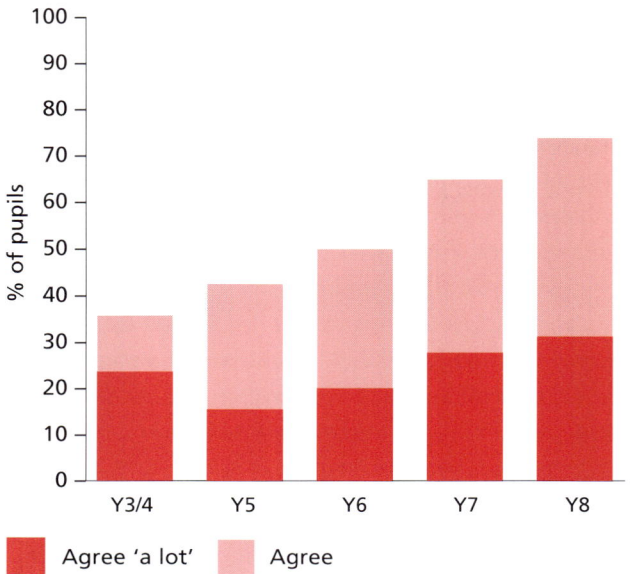

Ns= Y3/4:86; Y5:103; Y6:426; Y7:195; Y8:191

Source: OFSTED KS2/KS3 Pupil Survey, Autumn 1997

Pupils themselves seemed clear about the benefits of independent study, with a parallel trend for this attitude to emerge more clearly as pupils got older (Figure 4.2). The graph shows the percentage of each year group 'agreeing' or 'strongly agreeing' with the statement, 'I work better at home, on my own'.

Other patterns emerge from analyses related to Table 4.1. First, older pupils were more flexible about where they did their homework. While working at home was the norm, between a third and a half 'sometimes' worked elsewhere. In particular, they were much more likely than primary pupils to use school or some other organised study context on occasion. The trend for at least some pupils to work 'sometimes' in school seemed to start in Year 6, when almost a quarter did so, rising to over a third in Year 7 and over half in Year 8.

However, it is worth noting that over 40% of each group did their homework 'at another house' at least sometimes. What does this imply? The most obvious clues come from responses to another question about who helped pupils with their homework (Table 4.2).

Table 4.2
Sources of help with homework

People who help with homework	KS2 % of pupils	KS3 % of pupils
Mother and/or father	92	88
Brothers and/or sisters	33	41
Teachers	41	39
Friends	35	54
Grandparents or other relations	37	24
Did not respond to any item	2	2
N=	617	386

More than one answer could be given so percentages do not sum to 100
A total of 982 respondents gave at least one response to this question

Source: OFSTED KS2/KS3 Pupil Survey, Autumn 1997

Overwhelmingly, parents were the most obvious source of help, for pupils of all ages. However, it seemed that pupils were more likely to look for help from friends as they got older, with over half of the KS2 pupils doing so. It was also the case that girls were more likely than boys to turn to their friends, at both key stages. This, then, is almost certainly part of the explanation of why pupils were working 'at another house'; they were with their friends. However, the role of grandparents or other relations, and the mention by some pupils of going to a childminder's house while their parents were at work, underlines the variety of contexts in which homework was undertaken, occasionally or (for a minority) on a regular basis.

Comments from pupils who were interviewed at the case study schools supported and enlarged on the picture given by the survey on how pupils managed their homework. Most backed the system as a whole, seeing the gradual 'build-up' in the length and scale of tasks over time as a an appropriate approach, and often linking it with preparation for future ordeals - whether the demands of secondary schools or the rigours of GCSE. They explained that they found it easier to concentrate at home, away from friends, with older pupils usually working in their own room often with accompanying music (a very small

number mentioned parental bans on music or TV during homework time). In this, they echoed the practice of the young people surveyed through audience research, discussed in Appendix B (Wober, 1990, 1992). They valued parental support and help, although one Year 3 pupil pointed out that sometimes he could help his parents when they did not understand the work. KS1 pupils in particular enjoyed sharing tasks with parents, and the feedback they got from parents and teachers. At one school, pupils with SEN clearly enjoyed their equal involvement in homework, and the attention it brought them. The help given by parents was of many kinds, partly according to age, but often included testing (of learning), checking (of spelling and written work), factual information, help with research - using libraries and the Internet, setting up interviews with family members, finding relevant artefacts, and general trouble-shooting. They understood the difference between their own effort and the parent's role; as one Year 3 pupil put it, '*You learn on your own then get a grown up to test you*'. Another (Year 6) pupil felt the responsibility: '*If I get something wrong, it could be because I haven't explained to my parents what the work is about*'. But some pupils from large families explained how difficult it could be finding a place and time to work without distractions, let alone getting parental attention.

Staff explained that for some pupils the problems included one-room accommodation, absent parents, language difficulties and the extra tasks children were given. These could embrace not only shopping and childminding but also acting as interpreters for parents with little or no English. This meant they had little time to spend on their homework. This was a very different task load from that of other pupils whose lives were filled up with after-school clubs, sport, music and many other activities. But they too expressed concern and were glad when the school helped by sticking to a regular homework schedule. One secondary school which had set a '48 hour rule' (the time span for handing in homework) explained that if one evening was taken up with an event, this meant twice as much work the next night.

Indeed, time management was an issue pupils wanted to talk about. As some Year 6 pupils honestly explained, they knew it was a good idea to do their homework straight away, but they did not always get round to it. Those in schools with

Table 4.3
Sample Pupil Homework Timetables, Years 7 and 8

	School A Year 7	Year 8	School B Year 7	Year 8
Mon	Mathematics *Revision* German *6 sentences*	Art *Drawing* History *None* Science *Worksheet*	RE *Research* Mathematics *Questions* Geog. *Long/Lat Q's*	Science *Write up* French *Worksheet* Maths *Questions*
Tues	Mathematics *Revision* Science *Worksheet*	History *Research* Mathematics *None*	Music *Written theory* Geog. *Questions* Science *Revise - test*	Maths *Worksheet* Art *Draw eye/nose* English *Read*
Wed	Mathematics *Worksheet* History *Questions*	English *None* Mathematics *Questions* German *Revision*	History *Questions* French *Vocab. Q'ns*	Geog *Read study photo* English *Bookjacket* French *Learn vocab*
Thur	Art *Drawing* German *Sentences*	English *Prepare talk* Geography *None* Textiles *Finish fabric*	Art *Research* English *Write headlines*	Music *Project* Latin *Revise* History *Research*
Fri	History *Questions* Geography *Graph*	Mathematics *Questions* Geography *Revision* Technology *Write up*	History *Questions* Science *Revise*	History *Start questions* RE *OT questions* Geog *Revise*

clear and rigorously enforced procedures knew well what the penalties were and generally managed to avoid them. One Year 7 pupil in such a school pointed out that one of the purposes of homework was '*so you can organise yourself*'. Here early training helped; the only Year 7 pupil in the group who had not done regular homework at primary school found the most difficulty in complying with requirements.

The actual time and effort spent varied greatly, between schools, pupils and subjects. Even in the most systematic schools, there were weeks when homework was lighter because lessons had been taken up with tests. Moreover, the time invested depended partly on a pupil's interest and commitment to the topic. As we have seen in earlier chapters, many pupils enjoyed projects involving research and practical tasks, and could spend many hours on them. But ill-defined open-ended tasks ('*research the Big Bang and evolution*') merely caused frustration. Table 4.3

Table 4.4
Pupils' Attitudes to Homework (all year groups)

Views on school work and homework	Agree a lot	Agree	Not sure	Disagree	Disagree a lot
		Percentage of pupils agreeing			
My parents make sure I do my homework	54	33	7	4	2
Homework is important in helping me do well at school	52	32	11	3	3
I like reading on my own for fun	29	26	22	12	11
On the whole I like being at school	29	36	20	7	8
I work better at home	24	31	29	10	5
Sometimes I spend ages on my homework	22	39	20	14	6
Homework really gets in the way	14	15	22	23	26
Working on my own at home is hard	7	15	22	38	18
I do not really do much homework	2	7	13	37	41

N=1001

A series of single response items
Due to rounding errors, percentages may not always sum to 100
All respondents answered at least one item in this question

Source: OFSTED KS2/KS3 Pupil Survey, Autumn 1997

shows the homework tasks for a single week in two schools, for some Year 7 and Year 8 pupils. Although the tasks are only very briefly indicated, it is clear that there was a preponderance of written questions, learning, revision and reading. Moreover, even in these well-managed and demanding schools, homework was not always set.

In order to assess pupils' overall attitudes to homework and to school, those completing the questionnaire were asked to respond to a five-point agreement scale, running from 'agree a lot' to 'disagree a lot'. We have looked at one or two of these items already, but the full set of nine are shown in Table 4.4, for all respondents.

What made the analysis more interesting was to relate the answers to various other factors. For example:

- Girls were more likely than boys to:
    - like being at school (KS2 only)
    - work better at home (KS2 only)
    - like reading for fun

- Boys were more likely than girls to:
    - say homework gets in the way
    - not do much homework

- Those who enjoyed school were more likely to:
    - think homework important
    - work better at home (KS3 only)
    - spend ages on homework

Probably the most interesting changes were associated with age. Some of these were linear, representing a steady development as pupils get older; for example as we saw in Figure 4.2, agreement with the statement 'I work better at home, on my own' increased with each year group. Others were more complex, but there was a significant age-related effect for each of the nine items. The association between age and attitudes was summarised in an analysis of pupils' scores on underlying attitude factors. This showed that a positive attitude to homework and to school was strongest in Year 5 and (slightly less so) in Year 6. By Year 8, attitudes were apparently becoming more polarised, with minorities strongly committed to it or rather critical.

Figure 4.3 shows the percentage 'agreeing' and 'agreeing a lot' that they enjoyed school. Although well over half continued to agree this was the case,

enthusiasm was more muted after Year 5. In fact, only a fifth of the KS3 pupils agreed 'a lot' with this statement, compared with 44% of Year 5.

Figure 4.3
Percentage of pupils agreeing that, on the whole, they liked being at school: by year group

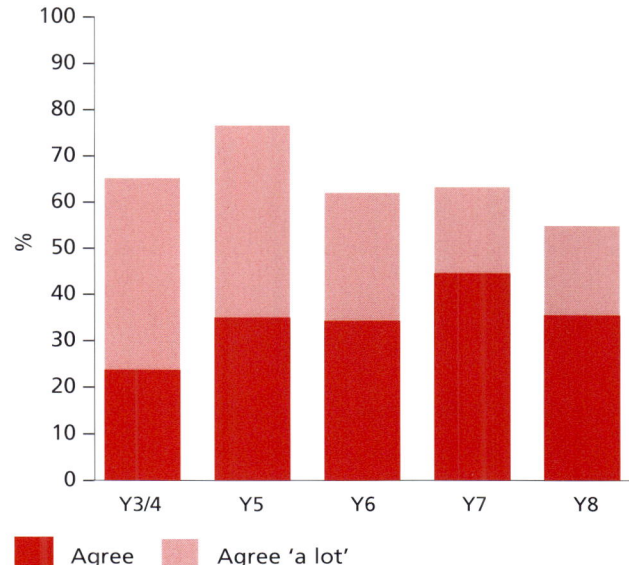

Agree   Agree 'a lot'

Source: OFSTED KS2/KS3 Pupil Survey, Autumn 1997

Analysis of the other factors underlying the attitude items suggested the ways in which attitudes change as pupils get older. Thus the idea that homework is hard, and working at home is more difficult than at school, was more likely to be found among younger pupils, while a factor linked to items suggesting homework could conflict with other priorities showed the opposite trend: it was older pupils who were more likely to express this view. This was perhaps partly explained by the fact that pupils apparently felt the burden of homework, in terms of the time they spent on it, more keenly as they got older; 80% of Year 8 pupils agreed that they sometimes 'spent ages' on their homework, compared with less than half of Year 5 (Figure 4.4).

Pupils' comments in discussion very often backed up the school's approach on the purpose and value of homework. One Year 6 pupil went as far as to say that having homework gave a school a good reputation and would help in getting a job. In general they appreciated that homework would probably help them with their class work. Even in Year 3 or 4, they distinguished between the 'boring but necessary' tasks or learning spellings and

Figure 4.4
'I sometimes spend ages on my homework'
by year group

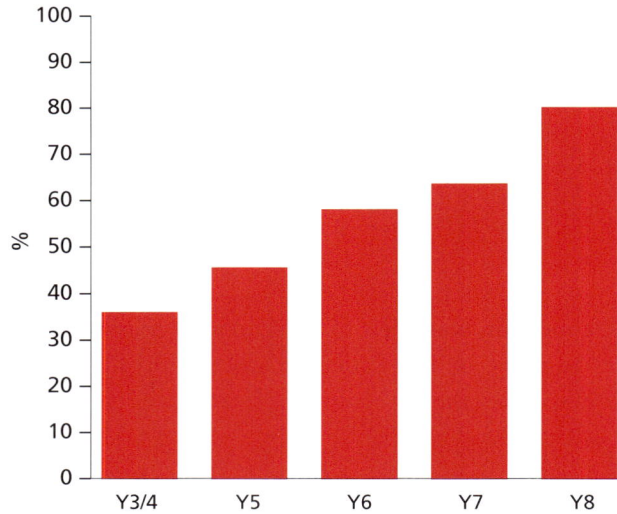

Source: OFSTED KS2/KS3 Pupil Survey, Autumn 1997

tables and the 'creative homework' of investigations which they really enjoyed. Some identified the intrinsic rewards - *'It's good to carry on using my brain'*. There was considerable pride in work well done, whether this was shown by getting full marks in tests, or by having work displayed and commended. However, poor management and feedback by teachers quickly had its effect in demotivating pupils. In one school they were described as 'unenthusiastic' about homework, complaining of too many routine, repetitive tasks and poor feedback in several subjects. Sometimes the difficulties were more individual:

> One lively Year 6 boy, whose problems with written work were well recognised (he worked on a hand-held computer), explained that he found homework boring, getting in the way of other things he wanted to do. He often rushed it, to get on to something better, doing the 'bitty' bits (learning tables, etc.) on the bus.

A Year 8 girl felt that teachers did not really understand how much time they were spending, and commented that the amount of homework she had been given in Year 7 had led to stress. Pupil comments also indicated where there were systematic discrepancies between policy and practice, in scheduling, marking or approach. For example in a number of schools, it was evident from pupil comments that 'finishing off' tasks were

more common than senior managers would have wished. Some of them recognised that the same task could make very different demands on pupils in a mixed ability class. However, few of the pupils we met had serious difficulties in completing their homework. Indeed, as one secondary teacher commented, pupils rarely told them about problems they might have at home, such as lack of space or family pressures. It was all the more important, therefore, for schools to establish effective communication with parents, so that they could both reinforce school policy and indicate where it was not working or was proving inappropriate to family circumstances.

Table 4.5
Problems with homework faced by KS2 pupils

Problems with homework	Often % of pupils	A few times % of pupils	Not really % of pupils	No response % of pupils
I don't understand what the task is	8	48	43	1
I can't concentrate	13	42	44	1
Teachers don't mark the work	11	43	45	1
I can't find enough time to get it done	11	37	52	0
I get stuck and can't get help	7	32	61	0
I forget to take my homework to school	7	37	56	1

N=386

A series of single response items
Due to rounding errors, percentages may not always sum to 100
All respondents answered at least one item in this question

Source: OFSTED KS2/KS3 Pupil Survey, Autumn 1997

KS3 pupils were asked specifically about some of the problems they might face in doing their homework. Their replies suggested that, on the whole, most pupils did not find the process problematic (Table 4.5). In each case, over 40% of them did not really experience difficulty. There was some increase in perceived problems from Year 7 to Year 8, associated with teachers' marking and help, but numbers were still relatively small. However, there was a minority of pupils - about one-fifth - who reported several of these problems, and they perhaps represent the group that schools need to target. Analysis suggested that they were consistently more negative in their views about homework and school than other pupils, found working at home significantly harder, and were inclined to look for help from friends. They were also more likely to feel that homework got in the way of other activities. However, it was difficult to characterise the group, in terms of gender, age or home background.

Teachers felt that most of the problems faced by the minority of pupils who failed to meet homework requirements could be attributed to lack of parental support (particularly in primary schools) or other difficulties at home. The telephone survey quantified their views (Table 4.6).

Table 4.6
Difficulties faced by pupils at home: teachers' views

Main difficulties faced by pupils	Primary schools % of schools	Secondary schools % of schools
Inadequate support from parents	72	63
Cramped home conditions (nowhere to study)	53	78
Noise/constant TV	44	54
Other demands (e.g. caring for family members, needed in family business)	19	46
No access to home after school (no parent at home until late)	11	14
Inability to work without professional support	8	16
Other activities, cubs, music etc.	7	(3)
Lack of discipline	7	(3)
SEN	5	5
Disturbed home/ quarrels	(4)	14
N=	226	139

All schools agreeing that some pupils had difficulties with homework
More than one answer could be given; all responses given by at least 5% of schools are shown
Items in italics were suggested by respondents

Source: Diagnostics Telephone Survey of Primary and Secondary Schools, Oct. 1997

By the secondary stage, when pupils themselves took on more responsibility for their own work, other claims on their time were seen as important, although even here these might be related to the family. However, in evaluating these responses it

should be remembered that a number of teachers at the secondary schools we visited admitted that it was often difficult to get accurate information about pupils' home circumstances.

Parents' perceptions and involvement: primary schools

As we saw in Chapters 2 and 3, many secondary schools had made a major commitment to working in partnership with parents, not least on the matter of homework. However, it was in primary schools, and particularly in KS1, that close collaboration was seen to be crucial, if homework was to prove both practicable and effective. Direct evidence was therefore sought from parents of primary school children. However, many of the points they made about the management of homework were equally relevant to secondary schools and, indeed, some parents had children in both phases.

There were a number of common messages that came through from the discussions with parents that took place during visits to primary schools. In summary:

- **A homework programme does promote partnership**

- **Parents want to know what, when and how**

- **Managing homework is a challenge**

- **On balance, there are lots of benefits**

Parents at schools which had worked hard at their partnership spoke enthusiastically about this approach. They greatly appreciated being involved; interestingly, whatever approach the school had taken, the parents of those pupils were ready to back it, as long as they understood what the policy was and how it would benefit their children. What seemed to matter was the readiness of the school to explain the rationale for homework and, even more importantly, to devise effective ways of involving parents in implementing the programme. There was enthusiastic support for almost all the strategies mentioned in earlier chapters to communicate and collaborate with parents: dialogue through reading and homework diaries, workshops on reading and mathematics, guidelines on early literacy and numeracy activities, shared investigations, information about topics and schemes of work, advice on managing regular and open-ended tasks. The enthusiasm for a collaborative approach and the benefits it could bring for both parents and children came over clearly from the discussion in a first school where many homework tasks were practically based for these younger children (4-8) and relied on parental help:

- They spent more time talking with children, and knew more of what was being taught.

- They liked the open-ended tasks - these were very interesting and drew the whole family in, so all contributed. They were very impressed by the mathematics projects and didn't know it could be so much fun.

- Their children were proud because their work was valued by the school.

- Teachers were seen as sensitive; they had clever ways of encouraging the less keen, for example by modifying the task to appeal to the child's interests.

- Parents were very keen and complimentary about teachers (who listen) and school (with its strong aims), and appreciated advice on how to help at home.

At another school parents suggested that by working together through the homework programme parents and teachers could pick up any learning problems earlier and more easily. Parents stressed the importance and value of this two-way communication. They wanted information and progress reports from the school, but they also wanted to have an easy feedback channel to the teacher, whether written or face-to-face. They also liked it when information and advice was tailored as closely as possible to their child, or at least their child's class. But above all, what seemed to matter was that teachers valued their contribution (even if they might not have recognised the term 'co-educators') and shared with them their professional assessments of the child's progress.

Parents had plenty to say on the management of the programme. They wanted the school to give them clear and accurate information about both the schedule and the actual content of homework. One mother explained how she valued the homework schedule the school provided, showing dates when work was to be completed or tested. These she wrote onto the calendar, to help her

own planning, and felt that it would be very difficult to manage otherwise. Other parents at the same school explained how they too used the homework schedule as a planning tool, in order to fit work round other family commitments. At another school, parents explained how the regular schedule helped the children, with their support, to learn to manage their own time. Any information that the school could provide about what children were learning at school helped parents to see how the homework fitted in so they could target help (with gathering information or materials) appropriately. The parents taking part in these discussions who, being available during a school day, perhaps had a little more time to give to their children than those who were employed full-time away from home, also spoke of the organisational challenge which homework presented, however clear and reasonable the schedule. They felt they had to be very organised themselves in order to support their children at home and that a lot was expected of them. This was especially true for the parents of children with special educational needs who had difficulty in settling down to tasks. There was concern from some parents that the demands might prove 'disproportionate' for some children or families. It was important for the school to ensure that children who lacked adequate parental support would not be penalised in any way. There was no doubt, they said, that homework impinged on family life, since it meant finding both space and time for several children to work on different tasks. It was the very children who were most involved in a wide range of activities, school-based and home-based, who could suffer; it was hard to motivate a child who had been involved in after-school activities until 5.30 p.m. Indeed, some parents questioned aspects of school policy - for example tasks set for half-term or summer holidays. Some found it easier to organise study sessions at the weekend, while others felt the weekend should be free for family activities. But they appreciated overall planning, for example the increase in the amount and frequency of homework as children got older.

Whatever their reservations about some aspects of homework requirements, the parents taking part in these discussions were overwhelmingly positive about the benefits that their school's homework programme had brought, for them and their children. Not only did they feel much more involved in and knowledgeable about their children's learning, but they could see what it was doing for them. Parents explained how their children were motivated to work at home, and were acquiring good study habits early on. Above all, they felt the proof came with the move to secondary school, with parents saying their older children were well prepared for Year 7. This was one of numerous benefits listed by parents of Year 6 children at a primary school in the north of England:

● The children are proud of their achievements and projects are valued by others.

● The children are used to homework -it's a part of their routine.

● They know their work is valued in class - they get feedback on tests.

● There is nothing at secondary school that could faze them!

Evidence from the schools showed that it would be unrealistic to see these enthusiastic parents as wholly typical. For example, reading records supplied by one school showed that the contribution from parents ranged from the highly informed and committed to the barest record, with no comments. Teachers in these schools were well aware of the challenge of winning hearts and minds, and sustaining parental support. Busy, working parents were bound to find involvement in homework challenging and others were known to be living with pressures of many kinds.

Nevertheless, the discussions suggested the kind of support and co-operation that could be developed when partnership started from the early years at school, and the benefits this could bring. While there were numerous small changes sought by some parents, most felt the balance was broadly right, and they were happy to work with the schools to continue to improve their programmes. The theme coming through the discussions, overall, was the trust which had been built up between teachers and parents, and the fruits this was yielding in children's motivation and achievements.

4.2 The Impact of Homework: Teachers' Judgements

Throughout the report, the strong belief of all the schools involved in the value of homework has carried with it an equal conviction - even an assumption - that homework has a positive impact on pupils' learning and achievement. Indeed in schools with an established homework programme, which would probably include all secondary schools, it may well be seen as a necessity, so that it is easier to imagine the negative impact there would be if it was suddenly abolished. But how well founded were these assumptions? What evidence did schools have that their homework programme was not only working (that is, operating as intended) but also making a difference to pupils' achievements? As Appendix B demonstrates, it is actually very difficult to prove a statistical association between 'doing homework' and achievement, even in large-scale surveys, since 'time spent' is at best a crude measure and there are no widely accepted performance indicators of homework quality. Few of the schools we contacted had even attempted any systematic investigation of homework outcomes and were not in a position to undertake controlled experiments. However, primary schools in particular could evaluate the impact of recently introduced or revised homework programmes. Moreover, teachers and managers in all schools with an interest in the effect of homework were in a position to use their professional judgement to evaluate its impact. In pulling together their views, we shall use evidence from interviews and from the telephone survey on the impact of homework, particularly on pupils' achievements and their effectiveness as learners.

In the telephone survey, primary school head teachers were asked about the impact which the development of their homework programme had had on pupils' motivation, independent learning and achievement over the previous three years. For each of these aspects, over a quarter of the schools felt that there had been a major impact and almost all felt there had been at least some effect. Figure 4.5 shows the results for all three aspects, which produced a very similar pattern of response, suggesting that schools found it hard to distinguish between these outcomes.

Figure 4.5
The impact of homework on pupils: primary schools

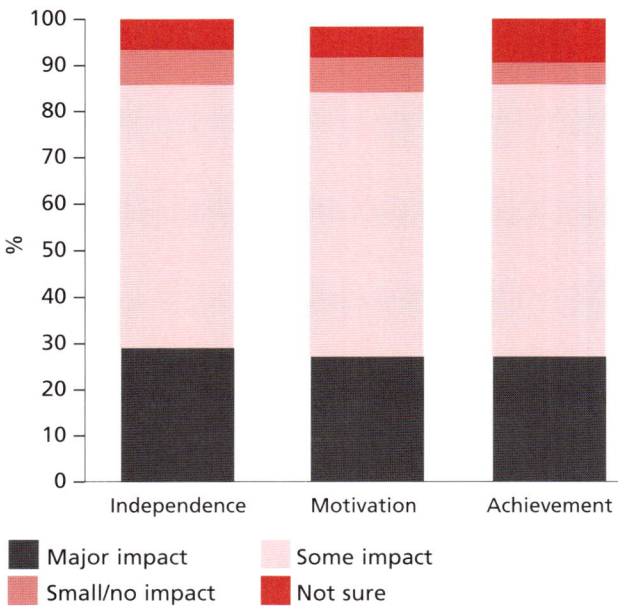

Major impact
Small/no impact
Some impact
Not sure

Source: Diagnostics Telephone Survey of Primary and Secondary Schools, Oct. 1997

Secondary schools were not all asked this question, since it was felt that many would find it hard to assess any specific effect over the last three years, but all those (43% of the sample) who had made any change to their policy or practice (usually by providing extra resources of some kind or setting up a homework club) were asked to evaluate the impact of this development. Here the results, based on this group, were more interesting than in the primary phase, in that schools were more likely to feel that pupils were now better at managing their own learning than that motivation or achievement had changed markedly. A further question about changes in parental attitudes, asked of both phases, suggested that there had been improvements in parents' knowledge, interest and attitudes to school. Almost all the primary schools thought that homework policy and practice had these positive effects; in secondary schools the link was less clear, with the possibility that other factors may have contributed to changes in parental attitudes.

During our visits to schools it was possible to get behind these general conclusions to ask about the **types of benefit** to pupils that teachers linked with homework. Only a few were prepared to commit themselves clearly to claims that homework had contributed directly to improved achievement outcomes, in terms of test or examination results,

since they recognised that many other factors might be involved. However, many schools were very ready to argue that, as a result of the homework programme, pupils were becoming more effective learners. Interestingly, primary staff were much readier to speak about the benefits which homework brought and the differences it was helping to make to pupils' learning, reflecting their interest in what was often a fairly new development. By contrast, many secondary teachers found it hard to imagine not having homework; its contribution was accepted as essential to the overall programme and, if results were good and improving, it could be inferred that homework was having the desired effect. The impact on pupils, as assessed by teachers, can be summarised under the three headings used in Figure 4.5 - attitudes/motivation, independent learning, achievement - with the addition of a fourth: increased time for learning.

Both primary and secondary teachers considered that a well-managed homework programme was an important tool in **strengthening the work ethic**. Pupils learned that work belonged at home as well as at school. Moreover, when the school had made it quite clear through its procedures that there were high expectations for homework, both for quality and compliance, this had an effect on pupils:

➡ At the technology college which had revised its programme, staff generally felt that the more formalised homework requirements, backed by the new discipline system, had brought significant benefits. Homework was more regularly completed and better integrated with class work, and pupils were more motivated to do their assignments.

In primary schools, it was reported, homework boosted pupils' confidence, and many blossomed with the additional one-to-one attention from parents and teachers. This was particularly true for pupils with special educational needs, in both primary and secondary schools which had taken care with their homework requirements. Some primary teachers were keen to point out that these attitudinal improvements were a dividend of the closer partnership with parents, which showed pupils that parents and teachers both understood and valued their work. Conversely, conflict and tension between teachers and parents over homework quickly had an adverse effect on pupils' motivation generally. Secondary schools stressed the importance of homework, as part of what one successful school called 'the school's ethos of working hard'. They pointed out that it was essential to establish this ethos from the start, so that pupils had developed the right attitude to independent study well before they embarked on GCSE courses.

One of the most significant and commonly mentioned benefits of a successful homework programme were **the habit and skills of independent learning**. Interestingly, this was seen as an outcome by teachers of all but the youngest age groups. Even for the latter, teachers explained how homework was establishing good work habits from the outset. In a primary school with many pupils living in cramped conditions, the head saw this aspect as very important: homework gave pupils opportunities for working out their own systems for doing things, and this was training for life. More specifically, pupils (with their parents' help) learned to make the hard choices about time management (e.g. balancing the demands of homework against social life and TV). Primary schools which had developed pupils' skills for managing their learning through progression in the design and completion of projects, book reviews or personal studies could demonstrate the impact of this approach in the quality of the work produced. Many primary schools linked pupils' ability to organise themselves with the effort made to prepare them for homework at secondary school. Such effort was not always recognised by secondary staff, who implied that it was the secondary homework programme which trained pupils in time management.

Better quality of work was one of the ways in which teachers judged that homework had contributed to **improved achievements**. As one interviewer at a primary school with a well-organised programme commented '*the standard of achievement [in homework] can be seen in the Year 6 projects on Europe - carefully researched, beautifully presented*'. But there were others. Several primary schools considered that homework had indeed contributed to measurable improvements in attainment:

➡ At a rural primary there had been an improvement in standards of attainment in KS2

tests (a target in the development plan), which the head associated with the new, formalised approach to homework.

➡ At the small 'book review' school, both NCA results and commercial test scores indicated that reading ages and mathematics performance were improving. This was an overall impact, not limited to one group.

➡ At a first school, the head felt it was possible to draw a direct link between NCA performance and homework; he felt it was striking that pupils who did not get parental help and support for their homework did less well in the tests.

➡ At another primary the head acknowledged that he could not separate out the homework effect as a factor in the improving NCA scores, although he sampled work every half term. But he felt that the regular practice in reading, spelling and tables improved performance.

Improvements in these fundamental literacy and numeracy skills through homework were mentioned by several schools, with particular emphasis on reading skills. One of the factors here, again, was partnership. Children were benefiting from regular and closely monitored reading. Teachers could see the benefit of their investment in collaborative approaches to early literacy development. The contribution which homework could make to skill development was also stressed by the SEN co-ordinator at a secondary school. But homework also helped pupils to improve their achievement by the opportunities it could provide for them to extend their interests, pursue work in greater depth and develop strategies which were generally impracticable in school (such as extended interviews).

Lastly, and to many teachers very importantly, homework created **more time for learning**. To secondary subject specialists this was often crucial; only by using homework time as part of the main learning programme could they cover their scheme of work.

➡ At a GM grammar school homework created about five hours a week extra learning time in KS3 and all staff thought that this was a very valuable part of the whole learning experience. In some subjects (science, for instance) it was seen as an essential part of learning time. In others, it was a way of expanding not just the breadth but also the depth to which a subject could be studied, which enriched learning.

But many primary teachers also appreciated the impact which this extra learning time had on pupil outcomes:

➡ At a primary with an established homework programme, teachers said that homework was becoming a more important part of the learning time available and without it time would have to created within the school timetable for routine tasks such as practice and reinforcement, and a certain amount of extension work. Little private reading was now done in school above KS1 although monitoring still took place, using the reading record. Focus group work with these readers developed higher levels of reading skills through work on texts in class. Homework time had therefore become essential and, as it increased, teaching and learning within the school had been re-directed to meet new challenges.

The simplest conclusion, drawn by several primary schools, was that by providing time for practice and reinforcement, homework liberated time for other teaching and learning activities in the classroom which more obviously required the teacher's professional skills.

Perhaps partly because homework was a new development in many primary schools, they were keen to identify its benefits, covering all the aspects we have discussed. Here is one school's list:

● Improved links with parents who have better understanding of their role.. and children enjoy sharing their knowledge and skills …. valuable practice.

● Extra practice time for skills development.

● Better assessment results at KS2 - children are better prepared.

● Checks transfer of learning into more independent situation.

● Motivates children to extend learning and to become independent.

● Strategies for time management.

● Takes some of the pressure off time in school.

But there was a **cost**: homework also had an impact on teachers themselves. They acknowledged the increased workload, but generally felt this was worthwhile. They spoke of higher expectations, sharper awareness of special educational needs, better organisation:

➡ At one 'very positive' primary school with consistent practice, the staff were seen as a tight knit group. They were all very committed and hardworking. Some felt they had become better organised through meeting the demands of the homework programme and that they now had more resources to tap. They felt they were giving better quality homework - they thought more carefully and matched tasks to abilities - and they also had to think about the circumstances in which the task would be completed. When they planned their class work they thought of homework that would complement it. It had an impact on their time and the amount of marking.

As we suggested in Chapter 3, the development of an effective homework programme, clearly shaped by and contributing to the school's learning policy, seemed to have the effect of increasing teacher commitment by demonstrating that they were all pulling in the same direction. However, senior managers were well aware of the need to have a 'finger on the pulse', to keep the system manageable.

4.3   Overview: the Impact of Homework

In this chapter we have looked at what KS2/3 pupils and parents had to say about homework, and the impact it had on their lives; and the impact which teachers thought homework had on pupils' learning. Most pupils in these 'good practice' schools generally seemed to have absorbed the messages they had been given on homework, and completed it without fuss. However, they and their parents were well aware that homework could be - and often had to be- fitted into family and personal life, and this might mean departing from school expectations about where and when tasks should be done. There was evidence of a growing confidence about working one one's own as pupils got older. However, other pressures emerged in KS3, and the sheer amount of homework was perceived as a burden; for a minority of pupils, homework brought problems of several kinds, problems which were not always made known to their teachers.

Both parents and pupils in the schools we visited were well aware that homework pressed more heavily on some families than on others, and showed a real concern about how these difficulties could be alleviated. A few schools had investigated these issues through parent or pupil surveys, but inevitably such an approach may fail to pick up the real problems. In general, schools perhaps need to monitor more carefully gaps of various kinds between school expectations and pupil behaviour, not relying so heavily on apparent compliance. We saw in Chapter 3 that there appear to be marked gaps between the time allocated to homework and the time pupils spend, with less time being spent on many routine tasks, while some open-ended assignments might take far more than the allotted time. While the timetable may be intended as a guideline rather than a prescription, how should teachers respond when pupils 'over-perform' in this way?

Teachers themselves were, on the whole, convinced of the value of homework, in improving pupils' motivation, developing the habits and skills of independent learning, creating more time for learning and - in some cases - visibly improving measured achievement. They were well aware of the cost to themselves, in preparation, marking and feedback, but those who shared a commitment to the homework programme were convinced the investment paid off.

5 Learning From Practice: Implications of the Study

In this final review, we bring together the findings from the whole report in order to suggest what we can learn from the schools we have studied about developing effective and manageable homework programmes(5.1). We also take the opportunity to consider the wider implications (5.2): what is the future of homework, within the broader framework of national policies to raise achievement and to promote lifelong learning?

5.1 Developing Good Homework Practice: Implications for Schools

We start with the implications for schools and focus on four areas highly relevant to good practice: the **foundations** on which the programme is built, the **integration into learning** of the programme, the **systems management** framework for implementing and sustaining the programme, and lastly the leadership challenge of **strategic development**.

Foundations

The common characteristic of effective homework programmes was that they were built on firm foundations. The programme had taken time and much consultation to develop; it was understood and endorsed by staff, parents and pupils; it reflected the school's overall philosophy and ethos; its purposes were clear and consistent. All this meant that programmes differed in their specifications, because each had been developed to fit the needs of a particular school at a particular stage in its development. But the process and parameters were broadly similar and were concerned with **partnership, principles and purposes**.

Partnership. The concept of partnership was seen as so fundamental by so many schools that it is in

danger of death from overuse. It is therefore important to be clear and realistic about what kind of partnership is needed for a successful homework programme. Often the stress is on partnership between school and parents, but, important though this is, there is also the issue of partnership among professionals within the school. Depending on the size and structure of the school, this may involve a team approach for the whole staff, co-ordination of internal subject or year teams, collaboration between class teachers and special needs teams and a collegial relationship between senior managers and other staff. In small schools where the whole staff team could plan and review policy together, developing the homework policy had actually strengthened the feeling of professional partnership. In larger schools, the same kind of cohesion was evident in some subject teams, resulting in agreed homework programmes. But success was more likely when the professional partnership was already strong; for example when the strategic and review role of senior managers was generally accepted by other staff as constructive rather than oppressive, and the system was open to ideas from all staff members. One or two primary schools which had won acceptance from the staff for the homework policy through a partnership approach felt that it would be important to make support for homework a criterion in interviewing candidates for teaching posts, and to include homework in the induction process.

The partnership with parents, relevant to all aspects of schooling, was widely recognised as crucial to the success of the homework policy. Some schools took a very strong lead and expected parents to follow it; this was particularly apparent in oversubscribed schools which had a *de facto* selection system. In some cases, parents were interviewed and the homework requirements were one aspect of the 'contract', formal or informal, which they accepted in return for their child's place in the school. Other schools were operating in a very different context where such an approach would have been inappropriate, either because of parental circumstances or because it was out of keeping with the school's philosophy. Such schools believed it was essential to win over as many parents as possible through persuasion and the experience of involvement. When policies were being developed, this could be challenging, and some schools accepted that the full partnership had to built up from the ground, with parents of new entrants. Nevertheless, it was possible to build outwards, too, ensuring that a core of parents were involved from the first stages of planning so that their perspective was incorporated into policy and practice and they could spread the message to others.

Schools were well aware that their parent body might include over-anxious or ambitious parents, who seemed to be more interested in rights than responsibilities and those who apparently had little time, inclination or skill for working with the school. Primary schools, however, could show that almost all parents were anxious to support their child, especially when they first came to school, if only the school could show them how to do this and provide the necessary encouragement and support. Secondary schools, too, could use the enthusiasm of the entry year to build the partnership with parents, through discussion and information. As we saw from the pupil survey, almost all the pupils thought their parents were firmly behind the homework policy.

Some schools felt that a contract was a valuable way of cementing the home-school partnership, in which homework was a key element. But others felt a contract was unnecessary or even threatening to the type of partnership they favoured. In either case, it was the quality of relationships which mattered; a contract was useful as a reminder of what had been agreed, but could not be a substitute for the hard work of partnership building.

In thinking about partnership, the pupils themselves must not be left out. While they may have no choice about being at school, equally the school has no statutory rights over their out-of-school time. It was a feature of the good practice schools that homework policy was built on relationships of trust and respect between pupils and staff. Pupils were trusted to complete their assignments, with parental backing; staff accepted the responsibility to set appropriate tasks and provide timely and relevant feedback.

Principles. Schools had to be clear about the principles on which their homework policy was built and to ensure that these were understood and accepted by all stakeholders in the partnership. It was perhaps too easy to assume, particularly in

secondary schools which had had homework for many years, that these principles were clear and non-problematic. In fact, as our interviews showed, there were certainly different emphases, even within one staff team. For primary schools, homework policies generally rested on the principle that it was educationally beneficial for parents to be involved in their child's learning. And yet many parents could probably recall a time when schools kept parents at arms' length, and were particularly opposed to 'interference' with the professional job of teaching the three Rs. Moreover, there could still be confusion, even in well-run programmes, about whether and how parents should 'help' with homework, once children got older. There were points of principle to clarify about the status of homework - for example, was it to be marked on the same basis as class work? - and about sanctions procedures which to some extent judged parents as well as or more than children. Was homework to be limited to assignments clearly linked to the classroom learning programme, or was the school endeavouring to use the homework programme to influence the kind of informal learning at home which can enrich children's ideas and develop their skills? Were the responsibilities of pupils, parents and teachers, and the way in which these would change as pupils got older, clearly defined? There was a risk that these important matters would be taken for granted or quickly summarised in the initial paragraphs of a policy, unless they were put on the agenda as part of the consultative process when policies were being developed or reviewed.

Purpose. We saw in Chapter 1 that most schools had little difficulty in setting out a list of purposes for homework, whether in their written policy statements or in interviews for a study such as this. Nevertheless, there were discrepancies between, on the one hand, the 'official' purposes expressed in these documents (or by senior managers), which were often concerned with such strategic aims as developing self-management skills, enriching understanding and consolidating home-school learning partnership; and the more pragmatic goals mentioned by teachers, such as creating more time to cover the syllabus, ensuring that practice and consolidation were catered for and enabling slower pupils to catch up with work they had not finished in class. **Unless the purposes of homework, and in particular the ways in**

which homework assignments grow out of and feed into the learning programme, are debated and agreed by staff, there seems to be little hope of realising them.

The point can be illustrated by one purpose on which most groups agreed: that homework should help to develop pupils' ability to manage their own learning - to plan, manage time, persevere, solve problems and so on. Was this actually a goal or just a hoped-for outcome? If it was a goal, then the school should try to promote it by teaching pupils, over time, how to develop these skills, perhaps by gradually increasing the pupil's responsibility for designing and managing their assignments - an approach being very successfully pursued in a number of primary schools we visited. Equally, schools could link homework with other initiatives to teach pupils how to manage their learning - for example, through mentoring, target-setting and study skills tutorials - as was happening in some secondary schools. What mattered was the congruity between the stated purposes and the programme developed to achieve them.

There will probably always be tensions about the purposes of homework. But if a school wants to design or redirect its homework programme in order to support its overall learning and attainment-raising strategy more sharply and directly, then it is clearly important to ensure that everyone involved understands how this may change homework objectives and practices. For example, while one of the purposes for homework in Year 6 may still be to prepare pupils for the requirements of secondary school homework, the first priority in these circumstances might be to maximise their progress in English and mathematics.

Integration with learning

Most of the schools we visited or surveyed wanted to ensure that homework was an integral part of the learning programme. This aim could be interpreted in rather different ways. For example, some teachers said if homework tasks were to be integral to the programme, then they had to arise naturally out of the day's work and could not be pre-planned. Some class and subject teachers also thought that control, over what homework should be set and when, was their individual professional responsibility and could not be shared. Most primary schools and some secondary subject

departments had developed a more strategic approach, which treated homework as one element of the whole programme of study, and also took account of progression within and across school years. This meant flexibility, to ensure tasks were appropriate for particular classes and individuals, and operated within an overall framework agreed by the teaching team. One primary head was thinking carefully about this balance, hoping to make the programme 'more manageable, less prescriptive, more flexible' within the common framework. In working for integration, the issues to be addressed can be defined as **planning, progression**, and **programming**.

Planning. Effective homework programmes involved a lot of careful preparation and planning. This took a number of forms, depending on the subject area and the age of the pupils. Using homework to develop literacy and numeracy in the primary years often meant constructing a scheme to support and complement what was done in class, and that applied to all the relevant age groups. Reading, spelling, number facts, handwriting: the programme for all these areas was planned by the teachers as a whole, using common published or school-developed materials and common procedures. The class teacher's responsibility was to use these materials to meet the needs of those pupils. A lighter touch was often applied to the planning of homework related to topics; however, some schools liked to ensure that each class teacher planned and published the homework assignments linked to these topics in advance. Some schools used published schemes for English and mathematics to structure the planning of homework for KS2 pupils. For a number of reasons, it was unusual to find a comparable attention to homework planning in secondary schools, but those who had undertaken planning as a department were convinced of its value. One effect of planning and publishing homework assignments was to give more control to pupils and parents, who could themselves plan ahead more effectively. Involving SENCOs in homework planning could have benefits for all pupils, not just those with SEN.

Progression. Where homework programmes had been planned in advance to complement classroom learning over a sustained period, it made it far easier and more effective to manage pupils' progression through homework; not just in the amount of work they were given, but in the type of task and the skills required to manage it. For a number of reasons it was easier to see this process in operation in primary schools, but there were instances of the same process at work in secondary departments, perhaps most usually in more linear subjects such as mathematics or foreign languages. Progression in homework was most evident in the development of literacy skills, through the use of phonics or spelling programmes. Teachers could readily set differentiated tasks, for individuals or more usually for ability groups, based on assessment of current performance, and using the appropriate level within the same scheme. Learning of number facts and tables could be approached similarly, balancing a common method and relevant, differentiated content. If the same programme covered a whole school or key stage, the familiar disjunctions that can occur when children change classes and teachers could be avoided or minimised. Progression in managing learning was promoted in some primary schools by the common, graduated approach to personal studies or book reviews, again covering a whole key stage.

In order to meet the need for progression in relation to homework, teachers had to think about the way in which it was assessed. Of course it was important to reward diligence and enthusiasm in completing homework, with praise and (in some cases) merit systems. But it was equally important to demonstrate that work done at home mattered just as much as class work. Applying the school's assessment policy, so that in general homework and class work were assessed on the same criteria, was one way of showing this. Moreover, as a number of teachers pointed out, some pupils surprised them with the quality of work they could produce at home - and they maintained they could tell when parents had taken too much of a hand. Equally important were the speed and quality of feedback, whether to individuals or to the class.

Programming. By programming we mean the broader agenda of scheduling, support and provision which are needed to back up homework planning and give teachers the best possible opportunity of using homework to enrich and strengthen learning. Primary schools often present homework as an overall programme, building up gradually from a small core in Reception. The programme often has a regular format for all

classes, at least for the core activities linked to literacy and numeracy, with a common spelling or tables day each week and a common framework for structuring longer tasks. To make it work, however, other resources are needed. These may include library and textbooks, access to computers, provision of notebooks, reading records and so on. But most importantly it means equipping parents with the information and guidance to work effectively with their children - a process to which committed schools have devoted much time, effort and imagination.

In secondary schools, programming focuses on the homework timetable, which attempts to allocate time fairly across all subjects. It is clear that in many schools the operation of this timetable is not quite as straightforward as it appears, since subject specialists often want greater flexibility than it provides, while senior managers and tutors want to ensure that pupils have a proper balance of subjects and daily allocations. The programme can therefore sometimes seem more like a patchwork of competing claims than a coherent programme of skill development and sustained, challenging assignments. Coherence can be increased by consistency in other aspects of the programming, for example in assessment approaches, in access to resources (for example in provision of textbooks or use of computers) or support (through homework clubs or 'surgeries'). Lessons learned from the management of GCSE coursework would seem to be relevant to time management in KS3 homework: giving clear deadlines, complementing regular, time-limited tasks with longer assignments planned to run over several homework 'slots', and making clear to parents and pupils total weekly allocations for a subject. Backing up the homework programme with tutorials to improve study skills and time management has also proved valuable.

In structuring the programme, schools need to be clear about who controls it, and the criteria governing the arrangements; for example how time is allocated to subjects, or how and why decisions about allowing textbooks home are made.

System management

However educationally sound a homework programme is, its impact on learning depends on effective implementation: seeing that teachers, pupils and parents fulfil their responsibilities and that homework is set, completed and marked in line with the policy specification. In schools where the system was working smoothly it could be difficult to believe that this was a major challenge, but this was misleading; managers insisted that it depended on rigorous and vigilant monitoring. It also required excellent communication and a fair, consistent application of merits and sanctions. The requirements could be summed up as clarity, consistency and compliance.

Clarity. Homework programmes would only work well if everyone involved knew and understood exactly what was expected: the nature of the task, what the child had to do and - if relevant - how the parent was expected to help. The younger the children, the greater the need for clear and specific information for parents. Many of the primary schools took very great care to achieve this, by providing newsletters, timetables, topic outlines, written guidance and workshops. For the pupils, it meant ensuring the task was clearly explained and recorded by or for the child. Older pupils might have greater responsibility for knowing what was to be done and when, but it was still important for parents to know too - a responsibility which some schools took very seriously. Homework diaries and planners could be very useful for providing a clear record of tasks set and completed, but only if they were appropriately designed and properly used by teachers and pupils. Clarity about deadlines was also very important, and parents clearly appreciated the termly calendars provided by some primary teachers, showing the dates and deadlines for topic assignments. In secondary schools, requirements, like the timetable, were more complex, but some schools had laid down general rules. In principle, there seems to be no reason why subject departments could not provide guidelines as well as deadlines for some longer assignments in KS3, as they do for GCSE course work.

Consistency. Consistency proved to be a keynote of effective homework programmes. This was most obvious in the enforcement of procedures. There were clear rules and everyone enforced them,

saving a lot of energy otherwise expended in chasing up defaulters and trying to get work completed. The requirements might vary from highly structured procedures with a hierarchy of sanctions to systems that relied on persuasion and encouragement, but in either case everyone knew what was expected, regardless of which class or subject was involved. Consistency also applied to other aspects of the programme: the quality of presentation required and of feedback given by staff, rewards for good work, marking systems and the scope of tasks.

Compliance. It was the responsibility of staff to see that homework was set, completed on schedule, tested or marked and returned. Apart from a few schools where homework was seen as a voluntary activity, appreciated but not enforced, most staff took this responsibility very seriously. However, it was probably easier to manage in primary schools, once the 'good early habits' which teachers hoped for had been established. There were fewer assignments each week, compared with secondary schools; some of them were part of a regular weekly pattern of learning and testing and the class programme was usually under the day-to-day control of a single teacher. On the other hand, keeping up the daily routine of completing and exchanging reading records, and setting individual tasks and targets, could mean that each teacher had to supervise a complex programme of work. In secondary schools, effective compliance systems usually involved staff at all levels. Subject teachers were responsible for setting work and seeing that it was completed, while tutors had the task of checking diaries to ensure that work was set for all subjects, and that parents had checked that it had been completed. In effective systems, senior staff managed the monitoring process, using it also to check the quality of work set and completed.

Strategic development

So far what we have described has related to homework systems in a 'steady state'. There were a number of case study schools with established systems of this kind. It was in many ways more illuminating to visit a school where the policy had been developed or revised fairly recently. Senior managers were then able to explain why and how they had taken this step. It was clear that they saw the development as a dynamic process. They described how staff, governors and parents had been involved; some referred to a trial year and were anxious to explain how the homework programme fitted into their overall strategy for learning. In other words they were presenting homework policy as a dynamic aspect of the school's strategic development, which it was their responsibility as managers to plan and lead.

Four characteristics of strategic management will be considered, as they emerged from the study. In thinking strategically about the development of homework policy, managers recognised a responsibility to see that it was **context-specific, cost-effective and coherent**. They also knew they had to respond to **challenges** to the policy.

Context-specific. Head teachers stressed that they had developed a policy to suit their school and that it might not be appropriate elsewhere. At one primary school the head insisted that individual schools had to consider local needs and priorities and develop their own targets. She had worked in other schools where her current policy would be inappropriate. She also pointed out that developing a homework policy was a gradual and incremental process; hearts and minds had to be won, and attitudes changed.

The strategy had to take into account current home-school relationships and levels of staff expertise and experience. Above all, managers had to evaluate their overall strategy for learning and consider how homework would fit into it. The policy therefore had to be suitable for that particular school at that particular stage of its development. It also meant that, given the current pace of change, it would be unwise to assume that even a successful policy would remain effective and valid. Just as KS4 homework guidelines have had to change with the development of GCSE coursework, so new requirements and pressures might necessitate the review of current practice. The requirements of the new literacy and numeracy task forces, the development of target-setting, expansion of after-school clubs, growth of part-time employment - all sorts of factors, internal and external, could change the context and therefore mean that the policy would need review and revision.

Cost-effective. One of the less developed aspects of homework management was evaluation. Many schools monitored the operation of the system, but few had systematic procedures for evaluating its quality or the impact on learning. There were other aspects which were difficult to investigate because schools did not measure them. What did homework cost - in terms of regular staff time per week setting and marking, time on planning homework, extra time liaising with parents or supporting individuals, enforcement procedures, materials and equipment? Probably only the last would be readily costed. And what evidence was there that all this investment was cost-effective? What were the most effective time allocations, to secure the best learning outcomes? It was very difficult to judge. All that was clear was that teachers in many of these schools felt that the effort was worthwhile, judging by performance in the classroom and motivation to learn. However hard it may be to assess cost-effectiveness in these areas, schools might find it useful to define some relevant performance indicators, for evaluating progress and planning change.

Coherent. Homework policy cannot and should not be considered in isolation. If the aim of homework is to improve learning and help to raise attainment then it has to fit with other aspects of the school's learning strategy. At the same time, homework is only one aspect of the home-school partnership. So the policy should be congruent, on the one hand, with strategies for developing study skills and resource-based learning, assessment policy and differentiation; and on the other, with home-school contracts, behaviour policy and equal opportunities codes. While the underlying principles and purposes of the homework policy are common to all pupils, it has to cater for pupils' development as independent learners, perhaps from 5 to11 or 11 to18. This means that homework policy has be an integral part of the school's regular strategic review of the learning programme, as part of development planning, so that issues about its quality, purpose and contribution to raising attainment, and not just about its management, are kept under active consideration.

Responding to challenges. Even for schools with well-established homework programmes, nothing could be taken for granted; sustaining momentum was therefore seen as the key challenge for senior managers. One school illustrated this well:

➡ A primary school commended for its consistent practice where homework seemed to be 'part and parcel of the aims and ethos' recognised the challenge very clearly. Class teachers stressed that without parental support homework was not possible, and they therefore had to 'keep communication links open'; they felt there was a constant struggle against pupils' (or parents') lack of organisation. The head recognised that homework was a heavy burden on top of full-time class teaching and tried to help by taking all lunch duties. He also felt that teachers needed to reduce the time spent, by more advance planning and developing banks of tasks that could be used again.

It was evident that for many primary schools the challenge for their own staff and more especially in their work with parents, was to establish a homework culture - which most of the secondary schools we contacted felt had already been achieved. This concern was echoed in the telephone survey, with a third of primary schools mentioning the need for greater parental support; 17% talked about educating parents to understand the importance of homework. For secondary schools, those senior managers who identified a challenge were more concerned with better evaluation and finding time to assess its contribution to the broader aim of raising attainment. Here, it seemed from this study, there were further opportunities for working with heads of department on continuing review of the quality of homework planning and outcomes, in order to ensure practice was consistent with school and departmental goals.

5.2 The Future of Homework

In this report we have seen how schools' commitment to homework programmes which met the criteria used in the review above were generating reciprocal enthusiasm and support from parents and indeed from pupils. In practice, effective homework programmes were usually one element in a much broader strategy to improve all aspects of school life, and to respond to the many changes and developments taking place in education, inside and outside schools. Here we want to draw attention to this changing climate, in order to suggest how homework is being, and will need to be transformed, if schools' policy aims for it are to be realised.

Homework practice has evolved gradually, but there has been sufficient change in the last few decades for it to be worth presenting a 'before' and 'after' interpretation of its nature and purpose, in order to pinpoint the aspects which are most likely to need attention, if current good practice is to spread and develop to meet new challenges.

The 'before' scenario draws on practice as it was perhaps thirty years ago - a period when many adults now in senior positions were themselves pupils. At that time, homework was largely confined to the secondary phase and, within that, to grammar schools and the higher streams (and older classes) of secondary modern schools; the Newsom Report (1963) found that half of all the fourteen year-old pupils in modern schools did no homework. While many primary schools expected pupils to work on reading and spelling skills at home, and to learn their tables, few schools had formal homework programmes, until the run-up to the 11-plus selection process in the last year of junior school. Schools and teachers setting homework therefore had certain expectations about what pupils should be able to do. They hoped - and expected - that the parents of these children would share their view that homework was a necessary component of the programme, and would back up the school by seeing the work was done, in suitable conditions. Many parents shared with teachers an accepted view of what was involved: homework consisted in the main of clearly defined exercises, often using textbooks which contained all the necessary material and instructions, and which were issued to pupils (free) for the duration of the course. If pupils were at a school or in a class where homework was expected, then it was in effect compulsory. Homework was, generally, a finite set of school-controlled tasks, with little intrinsic connection with other home-based activities and interests. It was clearly distinguished from the wide range of extra-curricular activities which the school might offer, or sport, musical and other clubs that children might be involved with at home.

Many of these features of homework may still sound familiar, but the widespread introduction of homework programmes in primary schools has helped to alter the picture from the school side. The schools which have chosen to develop a homework programme for their whole age-range have naturally focused on a collaborative approach, in which teachers work with parents and children on learning activities they can share. While formal routines of practice and learning may develop, often schools encourage parents to accommodate these within everyday family activities which may be just as important in consolidating literacy and numeracy. In these and other ways the boundaries between 'homework' and other forms of study support and out-of-class learning become permeable.

At both primary and secondary levels, however, there are many other factors helping to change the context for and assumptions about homework. These include:

- **Family patterns.** The 'old' assumption was that mother would be at home to greet children and see that they did their homework. While this was perhaps never wholly true, changing work and family patterns mean that many (dual and single) parents will still be at work when their children come out of school.

- **Resources.** The role and use of the textbook has certainly changed, and is still under review. Textbooks are no longer the mainstay of homework. In part this may be a supply problem, and the alternative of photocopied worksheets may often be an impoverished substitute. But the range of relevant resources for independent study is changing faster than most schools can keep up with it; and, most importantly, through Information and Communications Technology (ICT) a growing number of pupils have direct access at home to a far wider and more readily updated range of resources, on every subject under the sun, than any teacher can possibly provide.

- **'Adults other than teachers' (AOT).** Under the 'old' pattern, homework was set and controlled by the teacher, with the parent as monitor. Now, schools are learning to draw on the skills of a wide range of adults, and seeing them as having a legitimate role in supporting learning. While parents are at the heart of this network, it also includes classroom assistants, mentors - both older pupils playing an 'adult' role and adults from business and the community, public librarians, youth workers and many others working with young people on school-managed 'homework' tasks as well as other forms of study support and extra-curricular activities.

- **Learning to learn.** While homework is still firmly attached to school subjects, as defined within the national curriculum, there is a growing recognition, in schools and in the wider community, that homework provides a prime opportunity for developing pupils' skills as **independent learners**. The key skills are those which are relevant to learning at all ages: for example self-management, time management, information retrieval, analysis, planning, structuring, and evaluation.

- **Government policy.** In the old pattern, homework was a matter for schools, largely outside the remit of government. Now, there are national guidelines for homework, to promote common principles and practice. The recent publication of *Extending Opportunity* outlines the Government's commitment to the development of all types of learning outside normal lessons, under the heading of study support. Homework is seen as one component within the study support framework. This, in turn, is presented as one strand of the broader strategy for raising the achievement of all young people. Finally, school learning is only one part of lifelong learning - starting in the home, and supported through policies for learners of all ages.

Within this broad context, planning for the future of homework is both challenging and exciting. Of course it is essential to work at improving the quality of current practice, even when this may be governed by fairly conventional assumptions. Ensuring that homework really supports and complements class work, is clearly defined, manageable and properly resourced, advances the learning of each pupil and is efficiently managed, is the immediate priority, and may provide the main medium-term challenge for many schools. But this does not preclude the development of a new and longer-term agenda, to promote progression in the skills of independent learning for all pupils, using all the current and emerging human and material resources.

In the future, it seems at least possible that distinctions such as 'class work' and 'homework' will be less important than concepts like group learning and independent study, both of which might take place in school, home or elsewhere with a teacher or without. Teachers remain at the heart of the process, because they, more than any other group, have the professional expertise and responsibility for developing children into effective learners throughout a crucial period of their lives. By working closely with others concerned with the same goal, they can build on the well-established bridgehead of the homework programme to exploit new thinking and new tools which are likely to enrich and strengthen that process, particularly for children who, in conventional terms would otherwise be most at risk of failure.

APPENDIX A METHODOLOGY

Evidence for the report was collected in Autumn 1997 from a variety of sources, including:

A.1 Research Review

Caroline Sharp of the National Foundation for Educational Research carried out a systematic review of research on homework covering the period from January 1988 to September 1997. The review provides an annotated bibliography of research into effective homework practices and their impact on pupils, parents and teachers. It covers some 60 articles dealing with:

- school practice
- impact on pupils
- impact on parents
- impact on teachers
- alternative facilities (eg homework clubs and libraries)
- resources for homework.

The review was restricted to research-based literature in English published or available in the United Kingdom.

A.2 Survey of schools

OFSTED commissioned Diagnostics Social and Market Research Limited to undertake a telephone survey of schools that, according to their inspection reports, had achieved above-average homework performance. A total of 468 schools were identified (280 primary and 188 secondary) of which 368 agreed to be interviewed (227 primary and 141 secondary). The interviews were conducted between 1st and 17th October 1997 by interviewers from IQ Field and Tab Ltd, working under direct brief from Diagnostics. Interviews were with the headteacher in primary schools and with the deputy head responsible for curriculum development in secondary schools. The survey was designed to obtain the following information from each school:

- the amount and type of homework set for each subject;
- arrangements for the assessment of homework;
- strategies used to encourage a positive attitude towards, and completion of, homework;
- pupils' backgrounds and attitudes to homework;
- parental attitudes and support;
- details of facilities available at school for pupils who were unable to work at home;
- the nature of the school's homework policy;
- measures for monitoring the impact of the homework programme;
- plans for future changes.

The survey results were analysed by NFER.

A.3 Case Study visits

HMI and OFSTED researchers carried out a series of case study visits to 19 primary and 10 secondary schools during the autumn term 1997. The schools selected were judged by inspectors to have successful homework policies in place. The case studies consisted of semi-structured interviews covering the following topics:

- homework practice (amount and type set);
- the integration of homework into the learning programme;
- pupils' responses to homework;
- resources and support for homework;
- the school's homework policy;
- the impact of homework policy and practice.

For the primary school case studies interviews were conducted with the following:

i. **Senior staff**

    Headteachers
    Co-ordinators of English and mathematics
    SEN co-ordinator

ii. **Class teachers of**

    Year 6
    Year 3 (if applicable)
    Year 2 (if applicable)

Reception (where the school had a home literacy/numeracy programme)

iii. **Pupils**

A small group (3-5) of pupils from year 6 and, where relevant and feasible, from a younger class.

iv. **Parents**

An informal group of up to 6 parents of children who are regularly set homework.

For the secondary school case studies interviews were conducted with the following:

i. **Senior staff**

Deputy Head (responsible for curriculum)
Heads of English and mathematics
SEN co-ordinator

ii. **Class teachers**

Year 7 and Year 8 tutors

iii. **Pupils**

Small groups (4-6) of pupils from Year 7 and Year 8

A.4   Pupil questionnaire

During the case study visits pupils from two classes in primary schools (usually years 5 and 6, but years 3 and 4 in a few schools), and from years 7 and 8 in the secondary schools, were asked to fill in a questionnaire. Separate questionnaires were completed for primary and secondary schools. In all some 1,003 questionnaires were completed. The responses to the questionnaires were then analysed by NFER.

APPENDIX B THE RESEARCH AND POLICY CONTEXT

What do we already know about homework? Two approaches to answering that question are considered in this chapter. The first (B.1) draws on the research evidence, to identify what has been learned, particularly in recent years, about the nature and impact of homework. The answers depend on the type of research questions that have been asked, and as we shall see there has been more interest in the quantity of homework undertaken than in the nature of the tasks or the purpose behind them. The second approach (B.2) is through consultation - in this case, using the responses from education professionals and other interested groups to the questions on homework posed in the 1997 White Paper.

B.1   Research on Homework

A review of research studies on homework, covering the period 1988-1997, but including a few key studies before 1988, was carried out for OFSTED by the National Foundation for Educational Research (Sharp, 1997). The comments which follow draw mainly on this review, which embraced international as well as UK studies. The aim in limiting the review to the last decade was mainly to ensure studies were up to date, although one earlier reviewer (Paschal *et al.,* 1984) was also dismissive about the technical quality of previous research. However, Sharp suggests that, even in recent years, Paschal's conclusion on homework research would stand, that '*surprisingly few methodologically adequate studies have been conducted*'.

Here we shall focus on five key issues and consider what the research evidence can contribute to our understanding of each one:

- the **purpose of homework**, at both primary and secondary schools and its **relevance** to learning in school;

- the **amount and type of homework** allocated to pupils at each key stage;

- the **processes for managing homework**, by teachers (planning, setting, getting it in, marking and feedback), pupils (recording, completing, handing in, getting feedback) and parents;

- the **resources needed** for homework, and **provided** by school, home and wider community including **parental involvement**;

- the **impact of homework** on pupils' learning, on staff, on parents.

The purpose of homework and its relevance for learning

Very few research studies have investigated the purpose of homework explicitly; it is more usual for its purpose to be taken almost for granted, with the research focusing on whether it is, or how it might become, effective in achieving its purpose. In fact, the survey undertaken by HMI in 1987, just before the period covered here, concluded that in order for the potential of homework to be realised, a clearer consensus was needed about the purposes of homework, implying that schools themselves did not always provide this clarity. An earlier review of studies about homework covering Canada, the USA and the UK (Zeigler, 1986) showed that parents wanted more clarity about homework policies and purposes than schools were providing. About the same period, a US research-based review (Palardy, 1988) discerned four main reasons given by teachers for assigning homework:

- to teach self-discipline, independence and responsibility;

- to increase students' academic achievements;

- to fulfil the expectations of students, parents and the public;

- to expand, explain and ease time constraints on the curriculum.

Research evidence suggested that the first of these was endorsed by teachers and principals and the last two more pragmatic reasons probably reflected practice.

In a later OFSTED survey of homework practice (1995), the purposes of homework, as set out by schools in their policies and as seen by teachers, pupils, parents and governors, were reviewed. Among the purposes cited by these groups, it was suggested that homework in primary schools:

- encourages partnership between parents and teachers;

- reinforces work covered in class;

- encourages pupils to develop initiative, self-discipline and study skills;

- prepares pupils for secondary schools;

- helps teachers to cover the requirements of the national curriculum;

- allows more effective use of taught time in school.

However, no information was given to show what weight was given to any of these purposes by any or all of the groups, except that the last two purposes were mentioned only in a small number of schools.

In secondary schools, it was reported in the same study that purposes were usually set out in a homework policy, and were summarised thus:

- to encourage pupils to work independently and be responsible;

- to emphasise the link between study and achievement;

- to consolidate, extend and prepare pupils for work done in class;

- to cover the requirements of the national curriculum.

Less information was given about the purposes which teachers, pupils and parents expressed, or indeed whether they knew and endorsed what was in the policy, since its implementation was seldom rigorously monitored. A major study of homework policy and practice in Scottish schools (MacBeath and Turner, 1990) suggested that parents and teachers were found to share a common belief in the value of homework, largely shared by pupils, with the main aim for all groups being the reinforcement of learning.

What seems to emerge from this rather slender evidence is that, at a very general level, all those involved usually see homework as actually or potentially useful in contributing to learning. Translating such general principles into practice is likely to be more problematic. For example, while teachers in a study of Scottish secondary schools wanted homework to reinforce learning, MacBeath (1996) suggested that in practice this was not happening in some cases because '*schools have failed to create a relationship between classwork and homework*'. Moreover, although schools, particularly primary schools, saw 'involving parents' as one of the purposes of homework, parents were often unsure how homework fitted in with wider out-of-school learning.

One way of overcoming these difficulties, suggested in several of these studies, was to ensure that all parties - teachers, governors, parents and pupils - were actively involved in defining and agreeing on the purpose of homework as a part of the process of developing a policy collaboratively.

The amount and type of homework allocated and reported

There is a considerable body of evidence, national and international, about how much homework is allocated by schools and undertaken by pupils (according to self-reports). This evidence covers **time allocation** (the amount of time to be spent), **frequency** (how often homework is set, overall and for specific subjects), **subject coverage** (the number of subjects or topics for which homework is set) and **tasks** (the range of types of work: written, learning, inquiry and so on). These different aspects are not always differentiated, or it is implied that one measure of volume is sufficient.

School specifications of homework volume. The 1995 OFSTED study of schools in England and Wales suggested that in KS1 most pupils spent 5-10 minutes a day (25-50 minutes per week) on homework (usually reading with a parent) and in KS2 the time spent per week on homework varied from one to four hours. These are broad limits, reflecting both the wide variations between schools and their approach: half the 58 schools involved in the survey did not specify how much time should be spent. At secondary level, too, wide variations were reported in the time allocated per subject, both between schools (in Year 7 from 20 to 60 minutes per subject on each occasion) and within

Table B.1
Frequency of Setting Homework in Mathematics and Science, Y9: TIMSS

Country	Mathematics Times per week				Science Times per week			
	None	<1	1-2	3+	None	<1	1-2	3+
England	0	4	91	5	0	12	86	2
Canada	2	3	24	72	4	20	55	20
France	0	2	11	87	2	34	60	5
Germany	1	1	22	76	3	41	43	12
Hungary	0	1	2	97	2	28	22	48
Japan	0	31	47	22	10	69	17	4
Scotland	0	24	52	24	2	66	32	0
Singapore	0	1	14	84	0	17	77	6
Sweden	0	26	71	3	-	-	-	-
Switzerland	0	23	30	67	4	46	41	9
USA	0	3	10	87	-	-	-	-

Due to rounding errors, percentages may not always sum to 100

Source: TIMMS, First National Report, Part 2, Tables 3.7 and 5.6
(Keys Harris and Fernandes, 1997b; drawing on Beaton et al., 1996b)

schools (for example, 80 minutes per week each for English and mathematics but only 40 minutes for science). The variation in time allocations between schools, particularly at primary level, was reflected in other recent reports (OFSTED, 1994; Barber *et al.*, 1997).

In international comparisons, wide differences have been found in the allocation of homework, using measures of frequency and time allocation, overall and by subject. The most recent evidence is for **mathematics** and science, from the Third International Mathematics and Science Study (TIMSS). This showed (Keys, Harris and Fernandes, 1997a) that mathematics homework was set less frequently to Year 5 (upper primary) pupils in England than in all but one (Netherlands) of the countries selected for comparison (Netherlands, Scotland, Canada, Hungary, Japan, Norway, Singapore and the USA); in the last five of the countries listed, the majority of pupils were given mathematics homework at least three times a week, while in England over half received it once a week at the most. (Just over a third of Year 5 pupils said they did not do mathematics homework.) No international evidence was collected from teachers on the allocation of **science** homework for this age group, but the pupil data suggests that 60% of English pupils in this

age group did not do science homework, a higher figure than for non-British countries. However, the picture was different for **Year 9 science** (Table 1.1): 88% of science teachers set homework at least once or twice a week, more frequently than most of the other countries. Teachers in Singapore set a similar volume of homework (i.e. total time allocation per week, based on frequency and time allocated per homework) but those in Hungary set it slightly more frequently. However, in **mathematics** England was still in the minority in setting less than three homeworks a week; in seven countries, over two-thirds of mathematics teachers set homework at least three times a week, although some gave rather short assignments; in Singapore the norm was three a week of over 30 minutes.

An American study building on TIMSS to compare mathematics and science practice in the USA, Germany and Japan showed that at age 13, US teachers were the most likely of the three to set homework in both mathematics and science. Using as the measure ' setting homework 3-5 times per week', the percentage of teachers doing this in mathematics were: USA 86%; Germany 75%; Japan 25%. For science the comparable figures were USA 48%; Germany 12%; Japan 4%. However, Japanese students also attended extra mathematics and science coaching out of school, no record being made of the total time this took.

Time spent by pupils. Many international comparisons, as well as some English studies, have measured the time spent on homework, as reported by pupils, rather than school or teacher allocations. This might be a total for all subjects or limited to certain subjects. For example, in the English study for TIMSS, Year 9 pupils were asked how much time they spent on all homework each day. This showed that 30% reported spending less than one hour, 55% spent one to two hours and 15% spent more than this. However, the question was put differently in other countries, making comparisons with English results difficult to interpret. Certainly, between-country comparisons based on 'time spent by pupils' rather than on teacher allocations could give rather different results. For example, in a large-scale study of primary pupils in the USA, China and Japan (Chen and Stevenson, 1989), it was found that US pupils in the equivalent of Year 6 were doing the least homework (four hours per week, for all subjects), followed by the Japanese (six hours), with Chinese children of the same age undertaking an astonishing 13 hours a week. In each case, parents were broadly happy with what their children were doing. In the UK, MacBeath and Turner (1990) asked pupils in Scottish schools about the time they spent on homework. Almost all primary pupils (Y5-Y7) did homework, up to an hour per night, but diaries kept by pupils for the study suggested that typically they spent five to fifteen minutes on English or mathematics each evening, with more time (20-30) being spent when there was 'project' homework. On average, just over half of the Scottish secondary pupils spent more than an hour per night on homework. In a study published in the same year, Plewis and colleagues (1990) found that in inner London primary schools, the median Year 1 child in the study spent less than 20 minutes per week reading aloud at home and 40 minutes per week with a parent focusing on learning outside school. The White Paper *Excellence in Schools* (1997) presented the results of an NFER study (Keys, Harris and Fernandes, 1995) which showed that almost half the Year 6 pupils did not expect to do homework each day, and only just over a quarter spent an hour or more each evening. By contrast, 71% of Year 7 pupils spent this much time. In 1993, similar questions

had been asked of Year 7 and Year 9 students (Keys and Fernandes, 1993), and at that time almost two-thirds of each age group reported spending an hour or more each day, with little increase for the older group. Girls appeared to be spending more time than boys. Barber *et al.* (1997) attempted to relate time spent on homework to school quality, as identified by OFSTED. This suggested that more time was spent in the 'commended' schools, but a number of problems with the design cast doubt on the validity of this finding. Internationally, however, less time is apparently being spent on homework than thirty years ago, at least by some age groups. One major review of 35 years of research by the International Association for the Evaluation of Educational Achievement (IEA) (Keeves, 1995) identified a marked decline in the time spent on mathematics homework in lower secondary school in all countries between the mid-1960s and the early 1980s. This was part of a trend for less time to be spent on homework in all subjects.

Given the differences between the scope, focus and methods in these studies it is difficult to identify clear measures of the amount of homework assigned and carried out, but certain patterns emerge which relate to this country. First, at primary level, children in England and Wales seem to spend less time on homework than their peers in many other countries; moreover, there is great variation between schools in what is expected. At secondary level, the differences between countries are less marked and in some cases (e.g. science) more time may be expected of English pupils, but there are still wide variations between schools. There are inevitable differences between the time allocated and the time spent, with girls devoting more time than boys, on average, and regular and possibly routine tasks being completed rather quickly. In general, the homework allocation increases with age. OFSTED (1995) reported about 30 minutes per assignment in Year 7, one hour per subject per week in Year 10, going up to 1½ hours in Year 11. In the same report, GCSE students reported working much longer hours than indicated in order to meet coursework deadlines.

Range of subjects and tasks. Apart from the TIMSS evidence for mathematics and science, and some work on reading, there is rather less information about the range and type of work pupils were given for homework than there is about the time spent. The 1995 OFSTED study reported that the predominant homework tasks at primary level consisted of reading practice and learning multiplication tables and spellings. But in secondary schools, homework was set in most subjects, with the week's homework timetable covering the curriculum. With the exception of reading, where there have been a number of studies of home learning methods (e.g. Brooks *et al.* 1996; Cuckle, 1996; Jones and Rowley, 1990; Topping and Whiteley, 1990), surprisingly little research seems to have been done on the range of homework tasks being assigned, within or across subjects. Attitudinal studies suggest that children are more motivated by assignments which require creative effort than by routine tasks, perhaps partly because the latter are more common.

Managing the process of homework

Very few of the studies focused specifically on the quite complex procedures which schools have to put in place to manage a homework programme effectively. The HMI reports on homework of 1987 and 1995 reviewed the procedures in place, including:

- school homework policies;

- procedures for setting homework, including homework timetables;

- procedures for ensuring that homework is completed;

- marking and feedback requirements;

- the responsibilities of teachers, parents and pupils;

- monitoring and review of the homework programme.

While they were confident, by 1995, that most secondary schools had a homework policy covering these procedures, concern was expressed that the effectiveness of these policies was rarely monitored by senior management teams. The position in primary schools was even less clear. In these reports and the Scottish study (MacBeath and Turner, 1990), there was some mention of homework diaries, which in primary school were being used to develop a dialogue between teacher and parent, while in secondary schools they

seemed to serve partly as a control mechanism, with parents expected to support the system by 'signing off' that homework had been completed. Instances of good practice were given, for example to demonstrate the value of rapid and specific feedback and clear information for parents about the homework programme. By contrast, MacBeath (1996) castigated schools for knowing little about the context of children's learning out of school. But the NFER review of research did not find any systematic studies of homework management programmes, or the effectiveness of mechanisms such as homework diaries, rewards and sanctions and parental workshops. A number of authors stressed the importance of integrating homework into the learning programme and teaching study skills, but there was little or no investigation of effective strategies for achieving these goals.

Resources and conditions for homework, including parental support

Although there has been sustained discussion in schools about the challenge of providing pupils with the books and other materials needed for homework, once again schools' provision of resources for homework has not been the subject of much systematic inquiry, with almost no mention in the studies covered in the NFER review. However, research carried out for the Educational Publishing Council (Johnson, 1997; Lambert, 1997) suggests that it is indeed an important issue. Answers to questions on the use and availability of books in six key subjects were included in a survey of over 4000 secondary school pupils in 22 schools (Johnson, 1997). Overall, only just over half the pupils had a book for their sole use in class, and only a third said they had books to keep (and therefore available to work on at home). The situation was most difficult in Key Stage 3, with major differences between subjects: well over half the pupils had a book to keep in mathematics, compared to a quarter or less in English and science. Lambert's pilot study in seven London schools related to one subject (geography) for one year group (Year 8) and was experimental in nature, investigating what happened if teachers were enabled to select all the books/resources they needed for a given topic. The study showed that most departments were chronically short of relevant texts and welcomed the experiment.

However, the findings, although tentative, suggested that supplying sufficient books for each pupil to have one was not, in the short term, sufficient to change established practice on resources for homework. Only two schools used the project to give pupils a text or atlas to work on at home, and in neither case did they apparently explain how it was to be used. In several schools, the books were taken in at the end of each lesson, even though they were not needed for other classes, and homework was still based on worksheets including material copied from the textbook. There were further implications for homework arising from the pattern of textbook use in class. In many cases, pupils were not encouraged or shown how to engage with the text in any sustained way; its use was heavily directed by the teacher. From this small study, it appeared that these Year 8 pupils were not well equipped to use a text on their own, except to complete closely defined tasks.

A study undertaken for the British Library (Children's Literature Research Centre, 1994) underlines this view, suggesting that many pupils in the 11-16 age range needed help in developing strategies for using non-fiction books effectively. In other words, even if they were allowed to take books home, many pupils might not be able to use them to good purpose.

In studies of out-of-school learning, reference is made to the importance of human resources - parents, other family and the local community - and the contribution these adults can make to children's learning. Most work has been done on parental involvement with reading, particularly with younger children. Interestingly, Plewis (1990) found that time spent reading on their own at home was a better predictor of pupils' reading progress than time reading to a parent. Several studies have looked at particular programmes of parental involvement such as the Kirklees Paired Reading and the Haringey projects. Jones and Rowley (1990) suggested that the success of the Haringey project was due to the level of structure built into the programme and pointed out that parental participation is not a single definable entity. Rather, it is a multi-dimensional process that warrants careful investigation in itself. Toomey (1993) argued that the key factor was the training given to parents so that they could intervene effectively when hearing their children read. The Kirklees programme used the technique of Paired Reading and trained parents to apply it, with apparently successful results. Drawing on another literacy development programme, in Sheffield, Nutbrown et al. (1991) argued that, conversely, teachers need to be trained to work effectively with parents, but there is no research evidence on how this might best be done. An earlier review, of homework practice in Canada, the USA and UK (Zeigler, 1986), suggested that many kinds of relatively simple parent training programmes are successful in making parents more effective home teachers.

One issue that has attracted attention relates to the ambience which young people choose, or tolerate, when they are doing their homework. MacBeath and Turner (1990) reported that both primary and secondary pupils commonly used loud music whilst completing their homework. Two audience research surveys carried out by the deputy head of research at the Independent Broadcasting Authority (Wober, 1990, 1992) suggested that many school pupils over 10 did their homework with the television on, with a substantial minority apparently finding this positively helpful. But most recognised that doing homework with the television on made it more difficult to concentrate.

One of the issues which schools have to address in planning their homework policies is how these can satisfy equal opportunities criteria. Little firm evidence was found in the NFER review on how schools have met this challenge, or indeed on the impact of efforts to overcome problems which some students face, particularly in their home circumstances. For example, no studies were found on efforts to satisfy homework entitlements for pupils with special educational needs; or on any issues affecting particular ethnic groups. As reported earlier, it is clear from surveys that girls are likely to spend more time in homework, but no other recent work on gender differences and how they have been approached in schools has been identified. The well-established finding, that attainment is positively correlated with social class and other socio-economic measures, is underlined in some studies of class-linked approaches to working with children at home (Martini, 1995; Elliott and Hewison, 1994). However, there are suggestions coming particularly from research on home-school literacy projects that training and collaboration can close this gap (e.g. Brooks *et al.*, 1996; Topping and Lindsey, 1991), at least in the short term, although the design of the research means the finding remains tentative.

Some of the special reading projects discussed earlier targeted individuals or schools deemed to be disadvantaged, in order to make 'homework' (broadly defined) more effective in itself, and to address the equal opportunities issue. Another recent approach has been to compensate for problems at home by setting up study support centres, usually based at or linked with school. MacBeath's (1993) evaluation of the Strathclyde Supported Study Initiative reviewed its impact on the schools selected because they served deprived populations. The evaluation was overwhelmingly positive: '*The enthusiasm of students and teachers for supported study exceeded most people's expectations*'. The perceived benefits for participating students included greater confidence, better teacher-student relationships, more effective study habits and improved grades. However, attempts to compare examination outcomes with a matched sample were inconclusive. Moreover, teachers were concerned about the lack of parental involvement, feeling that parents played a critical role, even in a school-based scheme. A review of other study support schemes, funded by the Prince's Trust (Prince's Trust, 1997) was also enthusiastic about their potential for enabling pupils in socially deprived areas in particular to realise the goals which schools set for their homework programmes. However, at the time of writing, no formal evaluation of these schemes had been completed.

The impact of homework on learning and achievement

The central issue of research on homework is whether it actually enhances learning, resulting in improved pupil performance. There is a considerable body of work on a number of aspects of this issue, in a variety of contexts, in the UK and elsewhere, but the results are inconsistent. This is partly because the question asked has varied, sometimes focusing on quantity (time spent on homework) and sometimes on quality of task and/or feedback. A meta-analysis of 15 studies undertaken between 1964 and 1980 and linking homework with achievement or attitudes (Paschal *et al.*, 1984) suggested that the outcomes were predominantly positive, with homework that was graded producing stronger effects. These effects were greatest for upper primary pupils. However, Palardy (1988) considered that the research evidence at that date was not encouraging: '*Although there are mixed findings... most research does not provide statistically significant correlations of homework with general academic achievement*'. Other researchers have underlined the importance -and relative rarity - of fast and appropriate feedback (MacBeath and Turner, 1990; Elawar and Corno, 1985).

Does more time on homework equate with more learning? The Chen and Stevenson study of homework in three cultures (1989) considered the impact on achievement and concluded that there was no **consistent** relationship between time spent on homework and academic achievement, **within** any of the three countries studied (USA, China, Japan). However, interestingly, when data was analysed **across** cultures, it appeared that children in cultures with longer homework assignments did obtain higher scores on achievement tests. Moreover, there was a motivational factor: the authors concluded from their analysis that if children were given interesting assignments, saw them as useful and said they enjoyed doing them, it seemed to facilitate academic achievement. Keeves (1995), reviewing six major IEA international comparative studies carried out in about 30 countries between the 1960s and the 1980s concluded that time spent on homework **across all subjects** is positively related to student achievement after other factors influencing achievement have been taken into account. Interestingly, this overall finding was not matched **within subjects**: for example, there were inconsistent results for science. Like Chen and Stevenson (*op.cit.*), Keeves points to student motivation as the possible explanation for these findings, but it is not clear whether the discipline of doing homework increases motivation, or simply that highly motivated students spend more time on it.

The recent TIMSS reports on mathematics and science all considered the link between homework and achievement, within and across countries, but again many of the results were inconclusive. The national reports for upper primary and lower secondary (Keys, Harris and Fernandes, 1997a,b) considered both the frequency of setting

Table B.2
Patterns of Association between Homework and Test Outcomes: TIMSS

Analysis level	Upper primary (Year 5)		Lower secondary (Year 9)	
	Mathematics scores	Science scores	Mathematics scores	Science scores
English national report: England only				
Homework in mathematics or science[1]				
Frequency	Positive[2]	Not asked	?Positive	Positive
Time spent	Unclear	Unclear	?Positive	Positive
Homework in all subjects				
Time spent	Unclear	Unclear	Positive	Positive
England and other countries: homework in mathematics and science				
Frequency	No association	No association	Not analysed	Not analysed
Time spent	Not available	Not available	Not analysed	Not analysed
International report (excluding England): homework (all subjects)				
Time spent	Curvilinear Most countries	Not available	Curvilinear Most countries	Curvilinear Most countries
	Positive Iran. Korea, Japan		Positive e.g. Korea, Romania	Positive e.g. Korea, Romania

1. *Primary school teachers were not asked in detail about science homework, but just under half the English pupils provided information on time spent. 'Frequency' here is binary: homework or no homework .*
2. *Many of the positive associations were slight, or explained only a small part of the variance.*

Based on Beaton et al., 1996a, b; Keys et al., 1997a, b.

homework and the time spent on it, linking these to achievement outcomes. The pattern of results is summarised in the Table B.2.

The table indicates where the patterns of positive association are. Briefly, in England, doing homework, or doing more homework, in the subject was slightly but positively associated with subject outcomes in mathematics at both age levels, and in science at Year 9. These findings initially suggest that homework policies and practices may be important factors in enhancing achievement. However, the primary results reported here had not taken account of other factors which might influence achievement, and each association was slight. The positive subject associations for Year 9 were matched by a link between score levels in the two subjects and the total time which pupils said they spent on homework each day. As with all such correlations, the result tells us nothing about cause and effect; we do not know whether pupils got higher scores

because they did more homework, or whether high achievers are given (or choose to spend) more time. The international comparisons are even more difficult to interpret. The primary mathematics link (based on frequency, that is, how often homework was set) did not hold up across countries (English National report). In the international reports, the starting point was different, since the input measure was time spent on homework in **all** subjects (not the subject being tested), and these analyses excluded England, where the question was asked in a different form. The most common pattern of association was curvilinear, that is, moderate amounts of homework time were linked with higher subject scores; spending either a lot of time or very little time was less productive.

The conclusion to be drawn from these studies is that it is very difficult to identify a clear 'homework effect', separate from the influence of all the associated factors such as home and family background which are themselves commonly associated with achievement. Moreover, frequency of homework or amount of time spent are relatively crude measures and do not address the key issue of quality: the relevance of the tasks set and the feedback given, the link between homework and learning programme, the resources and support provided. Qualitative factors of this kind have been included in some studies (e.g. Keys et al., 1997a,b), but again the results are not clear-cut. Very few studies suggest that homework has a negative effect on learning (although Laconte (1981), cited by Palardy (1988), concluded that homework for primary grade children was inappropriate and counterproductive). But identifying the factors within homework which make the essential contribution to raising achievement is a much greater challenge. The nearest approach, in the studies covered by the NFER review, was in some of the very detailed research on home reading programmes. These suggested that very careful planning, training for teachers, parents and any other participants, ongoing support and monitoring and close co-ordination between home and classroom learning were all important ingredients in success. It would be very valuable if future research investigations could focus more specifically on issues relating to the quality of homework tasks and programmes, and any links there may be between high quality and improvements in pupil performance. A related issue which merits more research attention than it has apparently received is the type and quality of feedback and its impact on learning, since there are some indications that this may be critical in helping pupils to benefit from their efforts.

B.2 The Policy Context

Until the publication of the 1997 White Paper, there had been remarkably little official guidance on homework, and certainly no statutory guidance, either in the 1988 or subsequent Education Acts, or in regulations or other instruments flowing from these Acts. There may well have been policy *assumptions* about homework, the purpose it serves and the kind of practice which schools should be following, but there were few explicit *requirements.* For schools seeking authoritative guidance, the most recent and relevant publication (up to 1997) would be the report from OFSTED

(1995), entitled *Homework in Primary and Secondary Schools*, which contains a number of recommendations and arose from a request by the then Secretary of State to look more closely at homework and the part it plays in raising standards. So the policy context for this study, that homework is (or should be) part of the agenda for raising educational standards, was already outlined during the lifetime of the previous government. What has changed is the determination to use homework much more explicitly as a tool for effective learning and, in particular, to expect all schools to apply best practice.

The publication of the White Paper set in train an intensive period of consultation, up to October 1997. One of the 36 questions to be addressed by those responding to the consultation focused on homework, and more particularly on the proposed guidelines:

- *What form should the homework guidelines take, and how can they be made most effective in practice?*

There was a very considerable response to this question, by LEAs and national organisations representing teachers, parents, governors, business and other interested groups, and the pattern of these comments is useful in indicating how practitioners view current homework practice and the ideas put forward in the White Paper. In general there was support for, or acceptance of, the policy approach. The principle of promoting homework as one element of effective learning was widely endorsed. There was more caution about the idea, and in particular the form, of national guidelines. Comments were made about certain aspects of the proposals and their perceived implications.

- **Status.** Respondents wanted to know what would be national and what local. Some wanted clear prescription from the centre; more hoped that national guidelines would set out a broad framework, leaving LEAs and schools flexibility to devise policies suitable for their context. A few spelled out doubts about the legal status of any homework requirements set out in national guidelines: should or could these be legally enforceable? If so, what would the sanctions be?

- **Scope, specificity and flexibility.** There was considerable discussion about the appropriate scope of the guidelines. This in turn was linked by some commentators to definitions of homework itself. At one end of a continuum, homework might be seen as a series of closely defined, time-limited tasks, rigorously controlled by teachers. As one LEA put it, '*homework should consist of closed tasks (except in exceptional circumstances) so that pupils know when it is finished*'. At the other, it could be treated as one element of the whole range of out-of-school learning engaged in by the child, or at least an opportunity to extend school learning in a flexible and creative way. Some felt that if the guidelines were to have any 'bite' it would be important to set down time allocations, graduated by age; perhaps these should be in the form of minimum amounts per day or week. But others felt strongly that this would be unhelpful; as one group put it: '*setting time limits may encourage teachers to set homework to comply with the rules rather than because it was educationally valid*'. One solution proposed by a number of LEAs was for the prescription to be devolved to local level. For example, the national guidelines could require schools to specify time allocations, perhaps based on specified criteria. These might be linked to proposals for home-school contracts, with guidance on time allocations or some other measure of quantity being set out in the contract. For example one LEA included in its proposals for the content of a home-school contract for primary schools four points on homework, including '*clear guidance on amount of homework expected (expressed as time each night/week) - increasing up to Year 6*'. However, a more common concern was about the dangers of focusing on quantity: 'quality not quantity' was a frequent refrain. These respondents wanted to ensure that national guidelines focused on the purpose of homework and how it would improve learning, rather than on the apparently legalistic question of how many minutes should be spent on it. Guidelines should aim to help all involved to ensure that homework was closely integrated with in-school learning and fostered pupils' capability, responsibility and independence. One suggestion, put forward by a number of commentators, was that the guidelines should discuss or define the purpose of homework in promoting effective learning, and how this changed and developed from 5 to 16. Indeed, another concern about the guidelines was how they could be framed to meet the needs of all pupils and all schools. Would separate guidelines be needed for primary and secondary schools, or for each key stage? Indeed, were guidelines really needed at all for secondary schools, where homework was well established? And how could the requirements of children with special educational (or indeed social or cultural) needs be catered for?

- **Audience and roles.** Who are the guidelines really for? Some commentators suggested that they were really for parents, and many had a number of points to make about parents' involvement in homework. One LEA went so far as to suggest that if the guidelines were for schools they were over-prescriptive or unnecessary: '*Teachers do not need to be told "what sorts of tasks make good homework"* '. More generally, it was thought guidelines should stress parental rights as much as responsibilities; for example, that schools should consult parents when developing policies, be clear in informing parents what was expected, provide workshops or other forms of support where appropriate and generally include them in a learning partnership. More specifically, it was suggested that parents could be given a list of homework tasks for the term or at least an outline of the scheme of work, and clear feedback on homework performance. But others accepted that schools would benefit from guidelines, and one LEA suggested three sets of guidelines: for teachers, for pupils and for parents. An idea emerging from various sources was that the guidelines should specify the criteria for schools' homework policies, and that these should clarify the roles and responsibilities of all concerned.

- **Resources and conditions.** Inevitably, it was suggested by some that lack of resources (books, materials, equipment) would render guidelines ineffective or irrelevant; or that the most important resource was staff time, in setting, marking and possibly supervising homework, and this was already under pressure. But a wider concern was about unequal access to resources, by certain schools or pupils, and how the guidelines would treat this issue. In many cases, the solution for pupils whose home circumstances made it difficult to undertake homework was seen to lie with the suggestions in the White Paper for study support centres, and a number of examples of current provision were provided.

- **Format and approach.** We have seen that there was strong support for a framework approach, by which the national guidelines would set out criteria or indeed a format of school policies. One LEA included their own guidelines for schools. One theme was the value of including in the guidelines examples of good practice, perhaps age-related, or of encouraging LEAs and schools to develop exemplar material. Another was that the guidelines should be very clear on principles and purposes, particularly the need to integrate homework into the curriculum. One commentator summarised a set of principles concisely: homework should be '*regular, revised, reviewed and integrated*'.

- **Implementation and management**. It was suggested by a number of commentators that no guidelines would be effective unless they covered the process of devising an effective strategy at school level: development, implementation and evaluation. Wide consultation was recommended at the development stage, to build a real partnership between home and school. Some spelt out rewards, support and sanctions that might be incorporated into the strategy. The need to include training, for teachers and for parents, was mentioned several times. A minority stressed the importance of regular monitoring and evaluation of any homework policy, recommending that this should be covered in the guidelines. One idea was to link this to the OFSTED inspection process.

Clearly, considerable thought had gone into these responses, suggesting that homework is already the subject of active discussion and development at local level and among education professionals. Indeed, one theme running through the comments was the hope that any national guidelines would be based on and seek to extend current good practice in schools.

B.3 Overview: Current Thinking on Homework

Much of the focus of thinking about homework in the past has been on the quantity of homework pupils are expected to, or actually do, undertake, rather than on the kind or quality of work this includes. While teachers and parents seem broadly agreed that homework improves performance, it is much more difficult to ascertain the key factors in this process. One theme running through a number of studies is the importance of motivation and commitment: if teachers, pupils and parents are committed to homework, the tasks engage pupils' interest and teachers provide rapid and relevant feedback, there is more likely to be an impact on learning. However, there has been relatively little research on how homework programmes can be made more effective.

The responses to the consultation suggested that there is now widespread commitment to the principle of homework for all, and that many schools are already working hard to develop their homework programmes to enhance learning. However, there are many practical challenges to overcome, and it is hoped that this is where evidence from practising schools will prove useful.

REFERENCES

BARBER, M., MYERS, K., DENNING, T., GRAHAM, J. and JOHNSON, M. (1997). *School Performance and Extra-Curricular Provision* (Improving Schools Series). London: DfEE.

BEATON, A. E., MARTIN, M. O., MULLIS, I. V. S., GONZALEZ, E. J., SMITH, T. A. and KELLY, D. L. (1996a). *Science Achievement in the Middle School Years: IEA's Third International Mathematics and Science Study (TIMSS).* Chestnut Hill, MA: Boston College, Center for the Study of Testing, Evaluation, and Educational Policy.

BEATON, A. E., MULLIS, I. V. S., MARTIN, M. O., GONZALEZ, E. J., KELLY, D. L. and SMITH, T. A. (1996b). *Mathematics Achievement in the Middle School Years: IEA's Third International Mathematics and Science Study (TIMSS).* Chestnut Hill, MA: Boston College, Center for the Study of Testing, Evaluation, and Educational Policy.

BROOKS, G., GORMAN, T., HARMAN, J., HUTCHISON, D. and WILKIN, A. (1996). *Family Literacy Works: the NFER Evaluation of the Basic Skills Agency's Demonstration Programmes.* London: Basic Skills Agency.

CHEN, C. and STEVENSON, H. W. (1989). 'Homework: a cross-cultural examination', *Child Development*, 60, 551-61.

CHILDREN'S LITERATURE RESEARCH CENTRE (1994). *Contemporary Juvenile Reading Habits: a Study of Young People's Reading at the End of the Century* (British National Bibliography Research Fund Report 69). London: British Library Board.

CUCKLE, P. (1996). 'Children learning to read - exploring home and school relationships', *British Educational Research Journal*, 22, 1, 17-32.

DEPARTMENT FOR EDUCATION AND EMPLOYMENT (1997). *Excellence in Schools* (Cm 3681). London: The Stationery Office.

DEPARTMENT FOR EDUCATION AND EMPLOYMENT (1998). *Extending Opportunity: A National Framework for Study Support.* London: DfEE.

DEPARTMENT OF EDUCATION AND SCIENCE (1987). *Homework* (Education Observed 4). London: DES.

DIAGNOSTICS SOCIAL AND MARKET RESEARCH LTD (1997). Homework Policy and Practice. Unpublished report to OFSTED.

ELAWAR, M. and CORNO, L. (1985). 'A factorial experiment in teachers' written feedback on student homework: changing teacher behaviour a little rather than a lot', *Journal of Educational Psychology*, 77, 2, 162-73.

ELLIOTT, J. A. and HEWISON, J. (1994). 'Comprehension and interest in home reading', *British Journal of Educational Psychology*, 64, 203-20.

HARGREAVES, D. (1984). *Improving Secondary Schools.* London: Inner London Education Authority.

JOHNSON, M. (1997). *The Use and Availability of Text or Course Books in Schools. A Report for the Education Publishers Council.* Keele University, Centre for Successful Schools. Unpublished report.

JONES, M. and ROWLEY, G. (1990). 'What does research say about parental participation in children's reading development?' *Evaluation and Research in Education*, 4, 1, 21-36.

KEEVES, J. P. (1995). *The World of School Learning: Selected Key Findings from 35 Years of IEA Research.* The Hague: International Association for the Evaluation of Educational Achievement.

KEYS, W. and FERNANDES, C. (1993). *What DO Students Think About School? Research into the Factors Associated with Positive and Negative Attitudes Towards School and Education.* Slough: NFER.

KEYS, W., HARRIS, S. and FERNANDES, C. (1995). *Attitudes to School of Top Primary and First-year Secondary Pupils.* Slough: NFER.

KEYS, W., HARRIS, S. and FERNANDES, C. (1997a). *Third International Mathematics and Science Study, First National Report. Part 2: Patterns of Mathematics and Science Teaching in Lower Secondary Schools in England and Ten Other Countries.* Slough: NFER.

KEYS, W., HARRIS, S. and FERNANDES, C. (1997b). *Third International Mathematics and Science Study, Second National Report. Part 2: Patterns of Mathematics and Science Teaching in Upper Primary Schools in England and Eight Other Countries.* Slough: NFER.

LACONTE, R.T. (1981). *Homework as a Learning Experience: What Research Says to the Teacher.* Washington, DC: National Education Association

LAMBERT, D. (1997). *Exploring the Use of Textbooks in Key Stage 3 Geography Classrooms: a Pilot Study.* University of London, Institute of Education. Unpublished report.

MacBEATH, J. (1993). *Learning for Yourself: Supported Study in Strathclyde Schools.* Glasgow: University of Strathclyde, Faculty of Education.

MacBEATH, J. (1996). 'The homework question', *Managing Schools Today,* 5, 7, 20-2.

MacBEATH, J. and TURNER, M. (1990). *Learning Out of School: Homework, Policy and Practice.* Glasgow: Jordanhill College.

MARTIN, M. O., MULLIS, I. V. S., BEATON, A. E., GONZALEZ, E. J., SMITH, T. A. and KELLY, D. L. (1997). *Science Achievement in the Primary School Years: IEA's Third International Mathematics and Science Study* (TIMSS). Chestnut Hill, MA: Boston College, Center for the Study of Testing, Evaluation, and Educational Policy.

MARTINI, M. (1995). 'Features of home environments associated with children's school success', *Early Child Development and Care,* 111, 49-68.

MULLIS, I. V. S., MARTIN, M. O., BEATON, A. E., GONZALEZ, E. J., KELLY, D. L. and SMITH, T. A. (1997). *Mathematics Achievement in the Primary School Years: IEA's Third International Mathematics and Science Study* (TIMSS). Chestnut Hill, MA: Boston College, Center for the Study of Testing, Evaluation, and Educational Policy.

NEWSOM REPORT. DEPARTMENT OF EDUCATION AND SCIENCE. CENTRAL ADVISORY COUNCIL FOR EDUCATION (ENGLAND) (1963). *Half Our Future.* London: HMSO.

NUTBROWN, C., HANNON, P. and WEINBERGER, J. (1991). 'Training teachers to work with parents to promote early literacy development', *International Journal of Early Childhood,* 23, 2, 1-10.

OFFICE FOR STANDARDS IN EDUCATION (July 1994). *Taught Time: a Report on the Relationship Between the Length of the Taught Week and the Quality and Standards of Pupils' Work, Including Examination Results.* London: OFSTED.

OFFICE FOR STANDARDS IN EDUCATION (1995). *Homework in Primary and Secondary Schools.* London: HMSO.

PALARDY, J. M. (1988). 'The effect of homework policies on student achievement', *NASSP Bulletin,* 72, 507, 14-17.

PASCHAL, R. A., WEINSTEIN, T. and WALBERG, H. J. (1984). 'The effects of homework on learning: a quantitative synthesis', *Journal of Educational Research,* 78, 2, 97-104.

PLEWIS, I., MOONEY, A. and CREESER, R. (1990). 'Time on educational activities at home and educational progress in infant school', *British Journal of Educational Psychology,* 60, 330-7.

SHARP, C. (1997). *Bibliography of Research Studies on Homework 1988-1997. Final report to OFSTED.* Slough: NFER. Unpublished report.

THE PRINCE'S TRUST (1997a). *A Breakthrough to Success. Study Support: a Review.* London: The Prince's Trust.

THE PRINCE'S TRUST (1997b). *Learning to Achieve. The Prince's Trust-Action's Study Support Evaluation and Development Project.* London: The Prince's Trust-Action.

THE PRINCE'S TRUST (1997c). *The Code of Practice Study Support.* University of Strathclyde, The Quality in Education Centre.

TOOMEY, D. (1993). 'Parents hearing their children read: a review. Rethinking the lessons of the Haringey Project', *Educational Research,* 35, 3, 223-36.

TOPPING, K. and WHITELEY, M. (1990). 'Participant evaluation of parent-tutored and peer-tutored projects in reading', *Educational Research,* 32, 1, 14-32.

WOBER, J. M. (1990). 'Never mind the picture, sense the screen', *Journal of Educational Television,* 16, 2, 87-93.

WOBER, J. M. (1992). '*Text in a texture of television: children's homework experience*', Journal of Educational Television, 18, 1, 23-34.

ZEIGLER, S. (1986). *Homework.* Ontario, Toronto: Toronto Board of Education.